D1123609

The Complete Book of
Quilting
PROJECTS & TEMPLATES

The Complete Book of
Quilting
PROJECTS & TEMPLATES

Diana Hill

THUNDER BAY
P·R·E·S·S

San Diego, California

Contents

Before You Begin

The versatile Log Cabin block, commonly used for quilt tops in the 17th and 18th centuries, is here enlivened with a feature block in the shape of a house.

A BRIEF HISTORY

Quilts are often described as 'snapshots in fabric'; they give us a picture of the time in which they were made and of the lives of the people who made them. Unfortunately, as most early quilts served functional as well as a decorative purposes, and were often reused as batting for different quilt tops or adapted for other purposes, few have survived intact. As a result, many of these valuable records have been lost. The recycling of such beautiful objects tells us something, however, about the frugality and resourcefulness of their creators.

The earliest form of patchwork was made for an Egyptian Pharaoh of the First Dynasty, in about 3400 BC. A type of patchwork also existed in the Middle Ages. At this time, worn sections of clothing were patched with other pieces, producing a layered effect. Clothing too worn to serve its original purpose was often used for bedding and patched over in the same manner. Over time, bed quilts became more decorative. Wealthy women began to take up quilting to show off their sewing and embroidery skills.

The quilting tradition

The patchwork quilt we are familiar with today was developed in England during the 17th and 18th centuries. The first types of quilts to emerge were the wholecloth, medallion and crazy patch quilts. The Log Cabin block was one of the most common pieced blocks used at this time for bed quilts.

The wholecloth quilt originated in Lindsey, in Suffolk, England. The original fabric used to make this quilt was composed of linen warp threads and wool weft threads. This combination of threads made the fabric heavy and stiff. Wholecloth quilts were stuffed with unbleached wool and were finely quilted with linen thread, to hold the loose batting together.

Whitework quilts made of cotton fabrics replaced the wholecloth linen and wool quilt a century later. Like the earlier wholecoth quilts, these cotton quilts had very thin battings, but they featured fine stitching, painstakingly executed.

Medallion-style quilt patterns were popular and cotton quilts with tops in this style were often used for wedding quilts. A frugal quiltmaker would often sew dark pieced sections on a plain background so that she could place either the pieced or the reverse side upwards and have the quilt appear as either a pieced or a wholecloth quilt. The lighter 'wholecloth' backing would be placed upwards in summer and the pieced, darker side upwards in winter. This system ensured that the quilt was turned over regularly and the sides wore evenly.

Patterned cottons, imported from India, began to appear in England in the 18th century. Fabric of this type, known as 'chintz', quickly gained popularity because of its bright, clear colors and pretty motifs. It soon replaced the heavier wool and linen cloth as the fabric used for clothing and furnishings.

The popularity of the imported cottons caused English manufacturers to fight against their import, and they became expensive and highly prized. Medallion quilts, consisting of central feature blocks, were an effective way to utilize precious left-over scraps of chintz. Pieces were appliquéd onto a square of plain, more affordable background fabric. The appliquéd square was then framed with a number of pieced or appliquéd borders until a suitable size was reached.

New technology

As mechanisation developed, good quality fabrics could be produced cheaply and in a greater variety of colors. Silks and velvets became popular for clothing and furnishings and scraps of these fabrics began to be used in crazy patch quilts. Large off-cuts of fabric were placed onto a piece of foundation fabric and the edges of the pieces of off-cut sewn down with fine embroidery to display a woman's fancy needlework.

A number of quilt-top designs have religious themes: The appliqué Rose of Sharon, representing the flower of the shrub *Hypericum calycinum*, has its origins in the Bible's Song of Solomon.

The 19th century saw a rapid increase in technological progress and educational reform in the West, which brought with it the invention of the domestic sewing machine and a recognition of the right for all people to have access to free education. This social and technological progress was a great boon for women and for quilting, which was invariably women's work.

The sewing machine, often a family's most treasured possession, freed a woman's time and allowed her to make more intricate quilting patterns, while universal education resulted in increased literacy. With this came an increase in publications such as newspapers, ladies' magazines and almanacs,which kept women in touch with quilting trends and allowed them to share information about quilting techniques.

The history of quiltmaking is an ongoing one. Over the years the variety of fabrics available to quiltmakers has expanded, increasing the range of colors and textures available and allowing quilters to use fabric much like an painter uses a palette. The biggest change in the last twenty years has been

the introduction of the rotary cutter and accompanying rulers and mats, which has allowed greater accuracy and speed. New techniques have emerged as a result. While the entire quiltmaking process is now often done by machine, the essence of quiltmaking remains the same. Like the quiltmakers before them, today's quiltmakers want a part of themselves to live on through their quilts so that in examining them subsequent generations will learn something about the lives and dreams of the people who created these beautiful coverings.

MATERIALS AND TECHNIQUES FOR MAKING QUILTS

Some materials and techniques for making quilts are described under the headings below. Not all the materials listed are essential, some simply make the work easier. Similarly, alternative procedures are included in the discussion of quiltmaking techniques.

Sewing machine

For the projects in this book, you will need a sewing machine in good working order that is capable of sewing straight stitch, zigzag stitch and blind hem stitch. These stitches are available on most modern sewing machines.

Before you start any project, give the machine a quick service. Clean out the bobbin with a brush or a lint-free cloth. Oil the machine, if it needs it, but don't over oil it. Remove the lint under the feed-dog plate, as this can dull needles and play havoc with the machine's tension. Put a new needle in the machine—a dull needle can prevent stitches from forming properly.

Sewing machine feet

For piecing, you need a foot that gives you an accurate ¼ in (6 mm). Most patchwork uses the imperial system but you shouldn't have difficulty finding a machine dealer that can provide an accurate ¼ in (6 mm) machine foot. For older machines, there are many feet that can be adapted. If you cannot acquire a ¼ in (6 mm) foot, place a ruler under the machine's needle and mark ¼ in (6 mm) from the needle to the right, then draw a vertical line at this point with a pen or with tape. Make sure the seam is accurate by sewing pieces together and then measuring the seam before starting a project.

For machine appliqué, you will need an open-toe embroidery foot or a clear, see-through foot so that you can watch the position of the needle.

For machine quilting, you will need a walking and a darning foot. A walking foot is used for all straight line quilting. It allows layers of fabric to move through the machine without shifting. A darning foot is used to do free motion quilting by dropping the feed dogs so that the quilter can manoeuvre the quilt in any direction.

Sewing machine needles

For general piecing, the best needle sizes to use for cotton fabrics are sizes 70/10 and 80/12. For machine appliqué finer needles are required (size 60/8 or 70/10). For machine quilting, use a size 75/11 quilting needle for thin and/or natural batt quilts, and a size 90/14 quilting needle for high loft and/or polyester batt quilts.

Sewing machine threads

Match the thread to the fabric when piecing. For example, when using 100 per cent cotton fabric, use 100 per cent cotton thread. Use a neutral color, for instance grey or cream, to match the tone of the background. Don't use a polyester thread for a cotton fabric: Over time it will cut through the fibres of the cotton. The same rule applies when choosing thread for machine quilting and mock appliqué.

Monofilament thread, which is transparent, is the most appropriate thread for quilt tops, as it takes on the color of any fabric that it is stitched or quilted over. Although made of nylon, monofilament thread has the elastic quality of cotton. Monofilament thread should be used as the top thread in the machine. A quilting thread that matches the backing fabric should be used in the bobbin. The top tension in the machine should be eased off so that the heavier quilting thread will anchor quilting stitches in the batting, or anchor appliqué stitches to the back.

Stitch length

When piecing by machine, the best stitch length is about 2.0 (this should produce twelve to fourteen stitches per inch). For hand piecing, you should aim to make about ten to twelve stitches per inch.

Rotary cutters

A rotary cutter is a round, razor-sharp blade attached to a handle, protected by a sheath. The best cutters have a U-shaped washer at the back of the blade which helps regulate tension. Many styles of cutter are available. The standard size blade is 1¾ in (45 mm). This is suitable for most cutting tasks but for cutting templates the most suitable blade size is 1⅛ in (28 mm). For cutting through four layers, the 2⅜ in (60 mm) or 2½ in (65 mm) blade gives best results. A cutter with a blade this size is also easier to hold, so it is suitable for those who find cutting a little difficult.

Rotary cutters are held in the hand in much the same way as a steak knife. The handle should rest comfortably in the palm and

Some of the materials for quiltmaking: Fabric, template plastic, sewing machine thread and pins.

the index finger should be placed on the top edge of the cutter handle. There is usually a ridged section in this area to help provide grip. The blade side of the cutter should face the body and cuts should be made away from the body, using a smooth firm motion, to provide control and to prevent cuts to the body.

Safety should be a priority when using a rotary cutter. The blade should be exposed only when a cut is to be made (this can be done with the thumb), and the protective sheath should be replaced as soon as the cut is finished to protect you and to prevent the blade from being damaged.

Rotary cutting mats

A cutting mat should be used with a rotary cutter to hold fabric in place and to protect the blade of the rotary cutter and the surface of the work area. Rotary cutting mats are made from self-healing plastic which allows cuts to mend.

The size of the cutting mat depends upon the size of the work area but the mat should be able to accommodate a quarter of the width of the fabric (or 11 in/28 cm). Bear in mind that the bigger the mat, the longer the cut you will be able to make. Rotary cutting mats should be placed on a firm surface, stored flat and kept away from heat, as this causes them to warp.

Rotary cutting rulers

Rotary cutting rulers are made of acrylic and are transparent. Designed to be used in conjunction with rotary cutters and mats, they have markings in ⅛ in (3 mm) intervals. To make the piecework quilts in this book, you will need a 6½ x 24 in (16.5 x 60 cm) and a 6½ x 12 in (16.5 x 30 cm) ruler. The first ruler is for squaring up the fabric and cutting long lengths of fabric for borders. The smaller ruler is for cutting smaller strips of fabric.

Square rulers, which come in sizes from 4½ square in (30 square cm) to 15 square in (100 square cm), are not essential. The larger sizes, from 12½ square in (80 square cm) to 15 square in (100 square cm), make it possible to cut large squares in one movement. The smaller 4½ (30 square cm) and 6½ square in (42 square cm) rulers are good for cutting blocks and trimming up.

Pins

Long, fine pins with heads that will lie flat against the fabric are recommended as they will go through layers of fabric easily, and allow you to sew up to and over them without the stitching puckering. Fine pins are preferable, as thick, large pins cause fabric to bunch up and piecing to be inaccurate. Pins should be placed at right angles to seams.

The Ohio Star block is pieced using square and quarter-square triangle units.

Scissors

You will need three types of scissors for quiltmaking: A pair of fabric shears or a pair of scissors to use exclusively to cut fabric; a pair of thread clips or small (approximately 4 in/ 10 cm long) scissors to clip threads when sewing; and a pair of scissors to use to cut templates from plastic and paper.

Template plastic

Durable, transparent template plastic is used to trace shapes onto fabric in much the same way as tracing paper. The advantage of template plastic is that it is much thicker than tracing paper, so it can be drawn around numerous times without the shape becoming distorted.

To use template plastic to create a fabric block, trace the block onto the plastic then cut the template out to the finished size plus the seam allowance.

Template plastic is often used for appliqué. Trace around the template with a marker on the wrong side of the fabric and cut on the drawn line.

Freezer paper

Freezer paper is paper coated with plastic on one side. To use freezer paper, trace the design on the side made of paper then cut out the design, making sure the cuts are smooth to avoid jagged edges being transferred. Iron the plastic side of the freezer paper template to the wrong side of the fabric. The heat of the iron will cause the plastic to stick to the fabric. Cut out the shape, adding a scant ¼ in (6 mm) seam allowance of fabric around the template. Snip any curves to within a few threads of the template to help turn over the seam allowance. Apply adhesive from a water-soluble adhesive stick to the seam allowance. With the fingers, press the seam allowance down. Use the pattern as a guide to place the appliqué piece on the background.

FABRIC FOR QUILTS

It is best to use pure cotton fabrics. Generally, all fabrics used for a quilt top should be of a similar weave and weight.

CUTTING FABRIC

Cutting strips

To prepare fabric for cutting strips using a rotary cutter, first iron the fabric flat. Fold the fabric in half along its length, and do this again, so that you have four layers. Make sure you fold on the warp threads (the threads that run down the fabric, parallel to the selvages). This may mean that the selvages do not align. Lay the folded fabric on a rotary cutter mat with the raw edge to the right if you are right-handed or to the left if you are left-handed. The folds will now be in a horizontal

position. Place a rotary cutting ruler over the fabric, at right angles to the folds and, holding it firmly in place, trim the raw edge with a rotary cutter. Leaving the fabric and ruler on the mat, rotate the mat 180 degrees, so that the newly trimmed edge is to the left if you are right-handed or to the right if you are left-handed.

Pick up the ruler, being careful not to move the fabric. Using the vertical measurement marks on the ruler, align the required measurement with the trimmed edge. Check the measurement by placing the horizontal indicators on the ruler on the fold and the double fold. When you are sure the measurement is correct, cut the first strip, then cut the remaining strips. Cut strips in batches of three or four, then turn the cutting board around to align and trim the cut edge of the fabric again.

Cutting shapes

To calculate the measurement for a square, add ½ in (12.5 mm) for the seam allowance to the finished size. To cut a square from a strip, open the strip to a double thickness only. Trim the selvage edge. Cut to the same measurement that you used to cut the strip. To check that the measurement is correct, align the 45 degree mark on the rotary cutting ruler with the corner edge of the strip. If it runs through the opposite diagonal corner, it is correct. Every third or fourth cut, realign the cut edge.

To cut a rectangle from a strip, repeat the procedure for a square, remembering to add ½ in (13 mm) to the finished measurement for the seam allowance.

To cut half-square triangles from a strip, calculate the finished size of the block required and add a ⅞ in (22 mm) seam allowance. Cut strips and then squares to this measurement. Cut once on the diagonal from corner to corner.

To cut quarter-square triangles from a strip, calculate the finished size of the block required, and add 1¼ in (32 mm) seam allowance. Cut strips and then squares to this measurement. Cut twice on the diagonal from corner to corner.

QUICK PIECING TECHNIQUES

Sewing on the line (SOTL) technique

This technique is used to sew a triangle onto a background rectangle or square when you do not want to cut out shapes that have to be sewn on the bias. Add a ½ in (38 mm) seam allowance to the finished size of the triangle. Cut out a square this size. Draw a line from corner to corner on the square, place in position on the square or rectangle, then sew on the line. Fold the excess fabric away to the corner.

Half-square triangle blocks

A half-square triangle block is a square that is divided into two

TECHNIQUE 2: MAKING HALF-SQUARE TRIANGLES

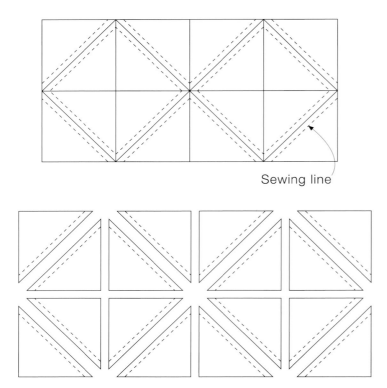

Sewing line

MAKING QUARTER-SQUARE TRIANGLE BLOCKS

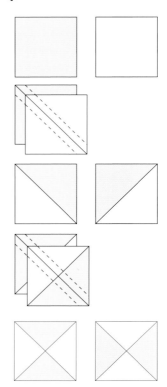

isosceles triangles of equal size. You can use either of two techniques to piece these blocks. To use the first technique, determine the sizes needed to cut the squares to make the block and add ⅞ in to the finished size of the block. Draw a diagonal line from the top left- to the bottom right-hand corner on the square that is the lightest color. Stitch ¼ in (6 mm) from both sides of the line. Cut directly on the line and iron towards the darkest color.

To use the second technique, cut out two rectangles of fabric. Mark a square grid on the lightest piece of fabric, making sure that your measurement is the finished size of the block plus ⅞ in (22 mm) and that you have at least ½ in (13 mm) around the outside edge of the grid. Mark a diagonal line across each of the grid squares. Sew ¼ in (6 mm) away from one side of the diagonal lines, then sew ¼ away from the other side of the diagonal lines. Iron the rectangle. Cut on the drawn lines. Then iron the seams towards the darker fabric.

Quarter-square triangle blocks

A quarter-square triangle block is a square that is divided into four isosceles triangles of equal size. One 90 degree corner of each triangle meets with the other 90 degree corners of the triangles in the center of the square. To determine the size of the squares needed, add 1¼ in (32 mm) to the finished size of the block. Cut two squares to this measurement, draw a diagonal line from corner to corner on the lightest of the squares. With right sides together, stitch ¼ in (6 mm) away on both sides of the line. Cut on the line and iron towards the

darkest color. This will make two half-square triangle blocks. Draw a diagonal line from corner to corner at right angles to the stitching on one of the half-square triangle blocks. Put both half-square triangle blocks together, making sure that you match opposite colors to each other. You should be able to feel the seams lock together. Once again stitch ¼ in (6 mm) away from both sides of the line. Cut on the line and iron in one direction.

Preparing bias binding for appliqué

Cut a square the desired measurement. Fold the square in half diagonally in each direction and press a crease in each of the folds. Cut along one diagonal crease. Sew two halves together with a ¼ in (6 mm) seam. Press the seam open. With a ruler, mark lines the required width. With right sides together and allowing a ¼ in (6 mm) seam, sew the fabric into a tube so that points X and Y match (see the Making Bias Binding diagram on this page) and the lines meet. Iron the seam open. Cut along the continuous line.

OTHER TECHNIQUES

Mock appliqué

Set the machine for blind hem stitch. The stitch width should be between ⅛ in (3 mm) and ¼ in (6 mm) and the stitch length should be about ¼ in (6 mm). Put monofilament thread in the top of your sewing machine and quilting thread in the bobbin

MAKING BIAS BINDING

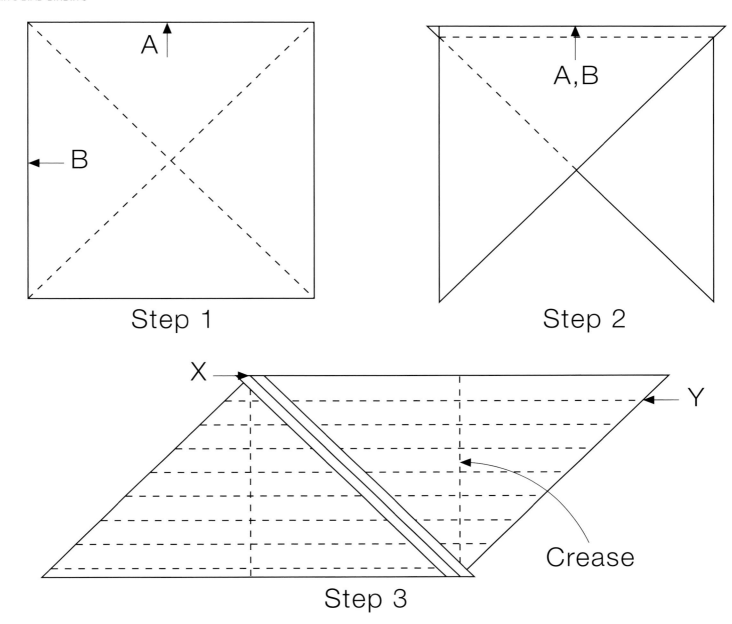

Step 1

Step 2

Step 3

and position the prepared appliqué piece on the background. The straight stitch component of the blind hem stitch should stitch into the background and the 'swing-over' component should catch only three or four threads of the appliqué shape. Pull the bobbin thread up and anchor with a few stitches in the same spot. Return to the normal position and appliqué the shape. End by anchoring again with a few stitches in the same spot. Clip threads to the surface.

Working from the back of the background square, using the stitching as a guide, cut a ¼ in (6 mm) inside the stitching, spray the area with water, wait a minute or two, and then remove the freezer paper from the appliqué by unpicking the seams. Iron the appliqué, from the back, and then lower the iron temperature and iron the front.

Appliqué

This method uses a heat-sensitive fusible webbing. Trace the appliqué shape onto the side of the fusible webbing made of paper and cut it out roughly, at least ¼ in (6 mm) from the outline. Iron onto the wrong side of the fabric. Cut out the design along the drawn lines. Remove the paper backing and place the appliqué in position on the background. Iron into place and machine stitch over the edges of the appliqué, using a small zigzag stitch. To stabilize the block and reduce the possibility of the stitches puckering, use a tear-away interfacing for the back of the block.

Foundation piecing

Foundation piecing is the method of making a block by sewing onto a piece of foundation fabric. Lines are drawn on the foundation to provide sewing guides. A paper-thin

interfacing without adhesive should be used for the base. Interfacing provides a firm base for the foundation patterns. It does not need to be removed when the quilt top is assembled, although it will add a little bulk to the finished quilt.

With a lead pencil, trace the patterns and markings onto the interfacing, allowing approximately ½ in (13 mm) between each pattern piece. Put numbers on the foundation pieces to indicate their sewing sequence. Cut the pieces out, not on the edge lines but out from them, to include the seam allowance. When piecing onto the foundation, sew one or two stitches over the edge line.

Place the fabric for the foundation piece right side up on the wrong side of the foundation, making sure the first piece is completely covered and there is allowance for a seam. Place the second foundation piece on top of the first piece, with right sides together, and stitch the seam on the right side of the foundation between the first piece and the second piece, making sure that the second piece is large enough to cover the area of the seam. Open up the second piece and press. Trim away any excess. (To ensure that the piece you intend to piece is large enough, pin the piece on the seam line and then move the piece open to check that it covers the intended area and there is allowance for a seam.) Place the third piece over the second piece with right sides together. Sew the second stitch line with the right side of the foundation facing you. Open the third piece and press. Continue following the numerical sequence indicated by the pieces. The construction of a foundation block is always the same, no matter how many pieces it is composed of. Pieces are always added in the order indicated by their numbers.

The foundation block has a ¼ in (6 mm) seam allowance around the edge. Work to the size of the finished block plus the seam allowance when you trim the pieced block. You may find, however, that the size of the finished block is ⅙ to ⅛ in (3 to 4 mm) larger than the edge lines indicate. This is because the bulk of the seams and fabrics have shrunk the size of the block.

Layering a quilt

On a table or a bench top, mark the center point of the quilt area. Put a button on this point and hold in place with tape. Fold the backing into quarters. Place the center point of the backing on the center mark of the work area and open the backing up (with the wrong side facing you). Make sure the backing is taut, then secure it in place by using clips or masking tape. Repeat the procedure described above to fold and place the batting and the quilt top. Smooth both out but do not hold in position with clips or tape. Using safety pins, and starting from the center point (you should be able to feel the button under the layers of fabric), pin all layers together. Close the pins when the whole surface of the table or bench is pinned. If the quilt top is bigger than the table or bench,

repeat the process by clipping the backing down on one edge of the work area and letting the weight of the already pinned middle section hold down the other side of the backing. Clip or tape the backing taut and continue pinning the quilt.

QUILTING

The following describes the procedure for machine quilting. All of the projects in this book can be quilted using this method.

Find the spot to begin quilting. Bring the bobbin thread up to the surface of the quilt and machine sew ¼ in (6 mm) of very small threads. Then quilt with stitches the normal length. When ¼ in (6 mm) from the end of the quilting line, again sew very small stitches. These small stitches will anchor the threads and prevent the quilting from unravelling. Clip all of the threads to the surface.

The quilting for most quilts is done 'in-the-ditch' (where the seams in the block occur). Because a seam is ironed in one direction, it has a high side and a low side. Quilting should be done on the low side of a seam, so that the stitching only needs to penetrate three layers instead of five, and will disappear.

Straight or walking-foot quilting should be tackled first. All layers of fabric must be anchored by quilting through the center, both vertically and horizontally. If you cannot stitch exactly through the center, anchor as close to the center as possible. Once you have done this, quilt from the center point to the border edge. Then turn 90 degrees and stitch from the centered anchored quilting line to the border edge. Repeat the procedure for the remaining sides until you have quilted all the straight lines. Then go back and ditch-quilt the blocks. For free motion quilting, change the foot to a darning foot and then drop the feed dogs. Follow the marked lines.

Scrappy Four-patch

Four-patch blocks, made of scraps of light and dark fabric, are used to create a simple, harmonious design.

This is the perfect quilt to make if you want to use up leftover pieces of fabric. It doesn't matter what color fabrics you have in your scrap collection, as every color in the spectrum can be used. Just make sure that you have both light and dark fabrics for each block so that you can create the striking tones that the quilt featured here displays. The instructions are for a lap-size quilt but you can make this quilt any size by constructing more four-patch units.

Finished size For the lap (130 x 130 cm; 51 x 51 in)

Materials
- ◆ 162 light to medium 2 in (5.3 cm) squares
- ◆ 162 medium to dark 2 in (5.3 cm) squares
- ◆ 100 plaid or floral 2 in (5.3 cm) squares
- ◆ 1 yd or 90 cm of cream self-print or plain fabric cut into 180, 3½ x 2 in (9 x 5.3 cm) rectangles
- ◆ 1½ yd (1.35 meters) of border fabric, to eliminate joins, or 1 yd (85 cm) of border fabric with joins cut into 5 in (13 cm) strips
- ◆ ⅙ yd (15 cm) of fabric for inner border, cut into four 1½ in (4 cm) strips
- ◆ ½ yd (50 cm) of fabric for binding
- ◆ 2⅓ yd (2.1 m) of backing fabric
- ◆ 1⅔ yd (1.4 m) square of wadding
- ◆ Rotary cutter
- ◆ Board and ruler
- ◆ Iron and ironing surface
- ◆ Dressmakers pins and safety pins
- ◆ Sewing machine

METHOD
1 Arrange the colored squares into sets of four: Two light squares and two dark squares.

Arranging the colored squares

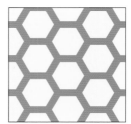

2 Sew two pairs of light and dark squares together separately, flip one pair and sew all the pieces together, allowing ¼ in (6 mm) for the seams, to form a four-patch unit. Press the seams.

RIGHT This small quilt is ideal as a blanket for the lap or for a baby's cot and would also make a pretty wall hanging or throw for a lounge chair.

Sewing light and dark squares

Sewing each unit

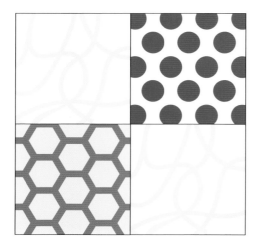

3 Sew eighty-one four-patch units.

4 Sew a 3½ x 2 in (89 x 50 mm) cream rectangle to the left-hand side of each unit. Sew a strip onto the right-hand side of the last unit in the row.

Sewing cream rectangles

5 Using plaids or florals, beginning with a square and ending with a square, sew 3½ x 2 in (89 x 50 mm) strips in between, so that you have ten squares and nine strips.

Adding plaids or florals

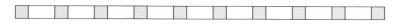

6 Sew the rows together, alternating the strips.

Sewing the rows together

7 Sew the inner border on the sides and on the top and the bottom. Sew the wider, second border, joining the pieces of fabric for the top, bottom and sides first, if necessary.

Sewing the inner border

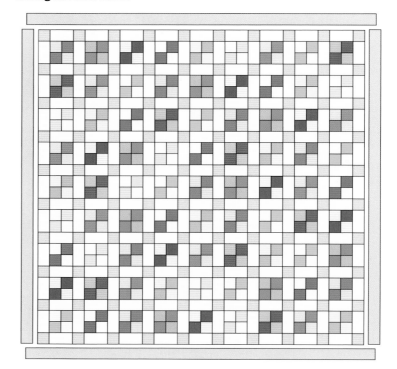

8 Lay the backing down wrong side up and place the wadding on top, leaving 2 in (50 mm) around the edges. Clamp the pieces firmly to a table and pin them together with safety pins. Machine quilt, or baste and quilt by hand.

9 Cut six binding pieces 2¾ in (70 mm) wide, join to the measurement of the quilt, and press with wrong sides together.

10 Align the raw edges of the binding with the raw edges of the quilt and sew ¼ in (6 mm) from the edge.

11 Trim the wadding and the backing back to ½ in (12.5 mm) from the stitching line.

12 Press the binding out and fold it over to the back of the quilt. Then slip stitch the binding to the backing fabric.

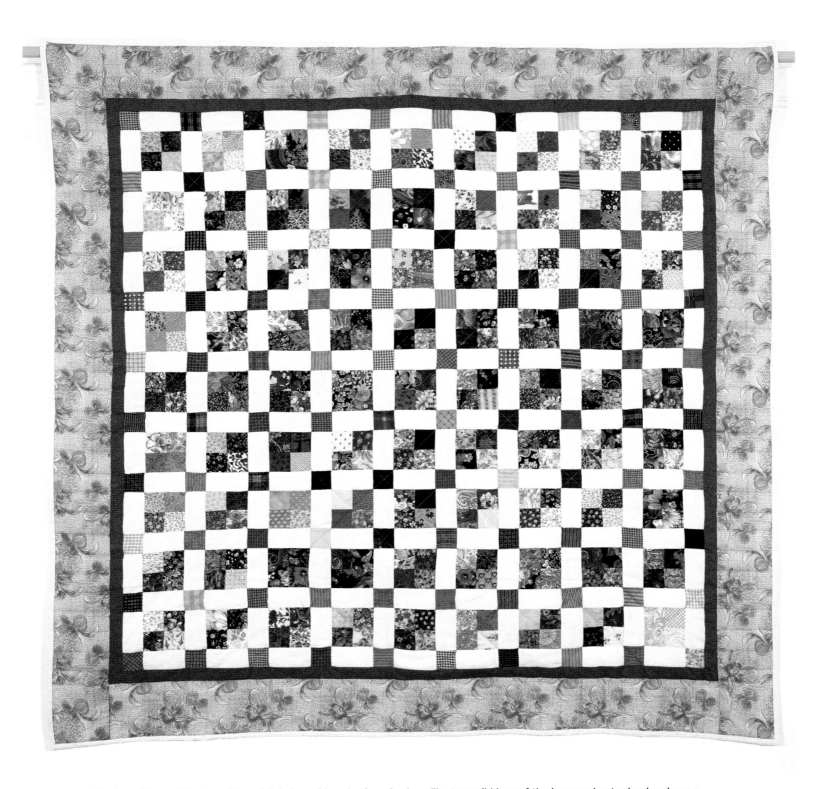

The top of the quilt is pieced from fabric in a wide selection of colors. The tranquil blues of the inner and outer borders have a softening effect on the busy scheme.

Fox and Geese

The quilt's angular shapes and strong colors give it a crisp, masculine quality.

Bow Tie blocks feature prominently in this traditional quilt design. The pattern is thought to have been developed by American pioneering women to depict the fate of their former homes. The diamond-shaped blocks represent geese, and the triangular shapes, marauding foxes.

Finished size For a single bed (135 x 203 cm; 53 x 80 in)

Materials

◆ 2⅔ yd (2.4 m) of cream background fabric
◆ 23½ in (60 cm) of a blue fabric
◆ 2 yd (1.8 m) of another, different blue fabric
◆ 15¾ in (40 cm) of a red fabric
◆ 31½ in (80 cm) of a different red fabric
◆ 7⅞ in (20 cm) each of two different green fabrics
◆ 3½ yd (3.2 m) of backing fabric
◆ 63 x 86½ in (160 x 220 cm) of cotton wadding
◆ Beige thread for piecing
◆ Blue and cream thread for quilting
◆ Rotary cutter, ruler and mat
◆ Sewing machine with ¼ in (6 mm) seam foot
◆ Safety pins

LEFT Simple white furnishings showcase the quilt's strong, geometric design.

CUTTING THE FABRIC

1 From the cream background fabric, cut five strips 2⅞ in (73 mm) wide. From these crosscut sixty-nine 2⅞ in (73 mm) squares. Crosscut these squares along one diagonal to form 138 triangles for piecing the blocks. From the same fabric, cut seven strips 2½ in (63 mm) wide. From these crosscut 108, 2½ in (63 mm) squares to use to piece the blocks. Also cut fifteen 2 in (50 mm) strips and from these crosscut two lengths of 11½ in (290 mm), twelve lengths of 10 in (254 mm) and forty-six lengths of 8½ in (216 mm) for the sashing between the blocks. Cut two strips 9 in (230 mm) wide. From these crosscut eight 9 in (230 mm) squares. Take two of these squares and cut along one diagonal to form four triangles for the corners of the quilt. Cut the remaining six squares along both diagonals to form twenty-four triangles used in the pieced edge. Cut one strip 4½ in (115 mm) wide from the cream background fabric. From this crosscut four 4½ in (115 mm) squares for the pieced edge triangles.

2 From the first blue fabric, cut two strips 2⅞ in (73 mm) wide. From these crosscut twenty-seven 2⅞ in (73 mm) squares. Cut these squares along one diagonal to make fifty-four triangles to use to piece the blocks and edge triangles. Then cut six strips 2 in (50 mm) wide for the first border.

3 From the second blue fabric, cut two strips 2⅞ in (73 mm) wide. From these crosscut twenty-seven 2⅞ in (73 mm) squares. Cut these squares in half along one diagonal to form fifty-four triangles to use to piece the blocks. Cut a strip 2 in (50 mm) wide. From this crosscut twenty 2 in (50 mm) squares for cornerstones in the sashings. From the second blue material, also cut eight strips 4½ in (115 mm) wide for the third border and eight strips 2¼ in (57 mm) wide for the binding.

4 From the first red fabric, cut a strip 2⅞ in (73 mm) wide. From this crosscut twelve 2⅞ in (73 mm) squares. Crosscut these squares along one diagonal to form twenty-four triangles. Only twenty-three of these triangles will be used to piece the blocks. Cut two strips 4⅞ in (124 mm) wide. Crosscut into twelve 4⅞ in (124 mm) squares. Cut the squares along one diagonal to form twenty-four triangles of which twenty-three will be used to piece the blocks.

5 From the second red fabric, cut a strip 2⅞ in (73 mm) wide. From this crosscut twelve 2⅞ in (73 mm) squares. Cut the squares along one diagonal to form twenty-four triangles of which twenty-three will be used to piece the blocks. Cut two strips 4⅞ in (124 mm) wide, then crosscut twelve 4⅞ in (124 mm) squares. Cut the squares along one diagonal to form twenty-four triangles of which twenty-three will be used to piece the blocks. Cut seven strips 1½ in (38 mm) wide for the second border.

6 From each of the green fabrics, cut two strips 2⅞ in (73 mm) wide. From these crosscut twenty-seven 2⅞ in (73 mm) squares. Cut the squares along one diagonal to yield fifty-four triangles to use to piece the blocks.

CONSTRUCTING THE BLOCKS

7 Collect the fifty-four triangles of each of the first blue and green fabrics. Stitch each blue triangle to a green triangle along the bias edge. Press the seams towards the blue pieces. Repeat this process for the second of the blue and green fabrics.

8 Gather the pieced squares made in Step 7 and the 108, 2½ in (63 mm) squares of the cream background fabric. Referring to the diagram below, piece together fifty-four four-patch units with two green pieces in the center, forming the shape of a bow tie.

Bow tie unit

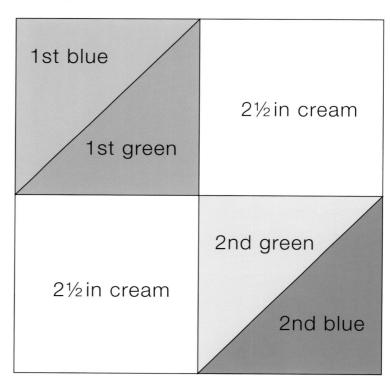

9 Collect the twenty-three 2⅞ in (73 mm) triangles of each of the first and second red fabrics and forty-six 2⅞ in (73 mm) triangles of the cream background fabric. Stitch each red triangle to a cream triangle along the bias edge and press the seam towards the red triangle. Trim the 'dog ears' at the corners.

FOX AND GEESE DESIGN

10 Referring to the diagram, with each of the pieced squares made in Step 9, stitch a cream 2⅞ in (73 mm) triangle to the remaining sides of the red triangle, to form a larger pieced triangle. Press the seams towards the cream triangle.

Red and cream triangle unit

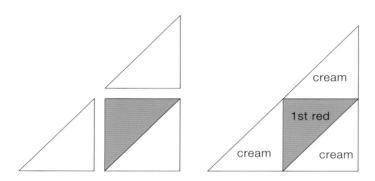

11 Separate the pieced triangles into those with the first red triangle and those with the second red triangle. To each of the units with a small first red triangle, stitch a second red 4⅞ in (124 mm) triangle to form a square. Press the seam towards the large red triangle. To each of the units with a small second red triangle, stitch a first red 4⅞ in (124 mm) triangle to form a square. Press the seam towards the large red triangle.

Red square

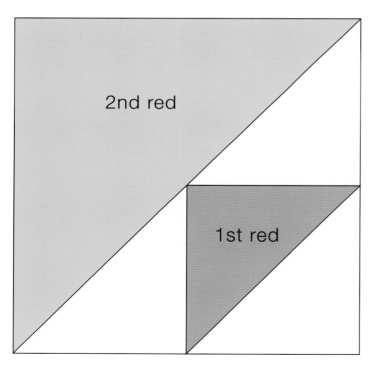

12 To form a block, take two pieced squares with the blue and green triangles and one of each of the red and cream pieced squares. The block is laid out in a four-patch

configuration with the two large red triangles in the center on the diagonal. The blue and green units are used as fillers, with the first blue triangles placed in the center of the block. Stitch the top two pieces together and press towards the red unit. Stitch the bottom two pieces together and press towards the red unit. Then stitch the middle seam of the block and press. Make a total of twenty-three fox and geese blocks.

Fox and geese block

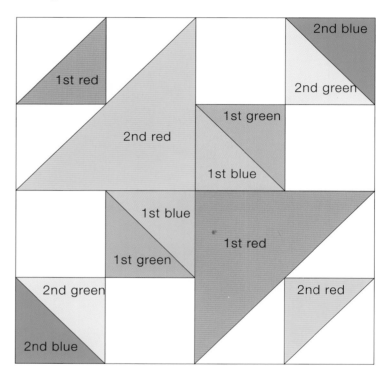

13 The edge triangles along the sides of the quilt are different from those along the top and bottom of the quilt. For the edge triangles on the sides, take the last eight blue and green units and sixteen triangles cut from the 9 in (230 cm) cream squares. Take a blue and green unit and place this down on point with the second blue triangle to the top. Take two 9 in (230 cm) cream triangles and

Constructing the edge triangles

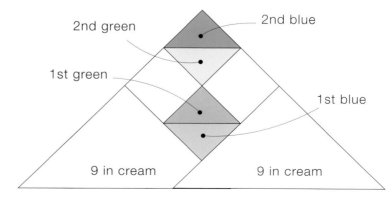

place these down on either side of the blue and green unit to form a larger triangle. Stitch a cream triangle to one side and press towards the triangle. Then stitch the second triangle to the other side, overlapping the end of the first cream triangle. Again press towards the cream triangle. Make eight edge triangles in the same manner.

14 Construct the triangles for the top and bottom of the quilt in the same manner but substitute cream 4½ in (115 mm) squares for the blue and green units. Make four of these triangles.

ASSEMBLING THE PIECES

15 Cream sashing strips are placed between the blocks with second blue cornerstones linking the blocks together. Start laying out the quilt by placing the blocks down on point, three block across and five blocks down. Leave space for the sashing between the blocks. Fill in the jagged edge with the side- and top- or bottom-edge triangles.

16 Place the sashings between the blocks. All the 8½ in (216 mm) lengths are used in the middle of the quilt, with the 10 in (254 mm) lengths used at the outer edges of the rows.

17 Piece the quilt top together in diagonal rows starting from one corner and working through the quilt. You will end up with rows of blocks and sashings, and rows of sashings and cornerstones. Stitch the rows together to form the quilt. Press all seams towards the sashings.

18 When all the rows are together, stitch the corner triangles to the quilt. These will be too large. Have an even amount of overhang on either side of a triangle and stitch to the quilt. Press the seams towards the triangle. Then trim back to level with the rest of the quilt.

19 The first quilt border is made using the 2 in (50 mm) wide strips of the first blue fabric. Measure across the quilt and cut two strips to equal the measurement of the quilt. Stitch to the top and bottom of the quilt and press seams towards the border.

20 Take the four remaining strips and join two strips together for either side of the quilt, using 45 degree seams.

21 Measure the length of the quilt and cut the joined strips to equal the length. Stitch to the side of the quilt and press towards the border.

22 Repeat this process for the second and third borders, using the second red 1½ in (38 mm) strips and the second blue 4½ in (115 mm) strips. It will be necessary to join strips to make the required lengths. Always press seams away from the middle of the quilt.

QUILTING
23 Cut the backing fabric into two lengths of 1¾ yd (1.6 m). Join these together along the selvage using a wide seam. Trim off the selvage and press the seam to one side.

24 Lay down the backing fabric, batting and quilt top. Baste the three layers using safety pins. Stitch in- the-ditch around each of the components of the blocks and the first and second borders. Stipple quilt using cream thread on the background. Use a cable variation to quilt the third border.

BINDING
25 Collect the eight 2¼ in (57 mm) strips of the second blue fabric. Join these end to end to make one long strip, using 45 degree seams. Press the length of binding in half with wrong sides together. Using a ¼ in (6 mm) seam allowance, stitch the binding around the outer edge of the border. Keep all raw edges even and mitre the corners as you go. Trim excess batting and backing fabric back to approximately ¼ in (6 mm) past the edge of the border. Roll the binding over to the back of the quilt and hand stitch in place.

The quilted curved shapes in the background fabric contrast nicely with the geometric pieces.

Winter Rose

Vivid Hypericum flowers, with yellow centers and dark green leaves, form the basis of the quilt's design.

This beautiful quilt, featuring a variation of the traditional Rose of Sharon pattern, will add appeal to an old-world bedroom. The flower motifs are appliquéd using freezer paper and blind hem stitched with a sewing machine.

Finished size For a double bed (200 x 200 cm; 78 x 78 in)

Materials

- 5½ yd (5 m) of white on white print cotton fabric (including binding fabric)
- 17¾ in (45 cm) of red print fabric
- 15¾ 9n (40 cm) of pink print fabric
- 4 in (10 cm) of yellow print fabric
- 1½ yd (1.35 m) of green print fabric
- 4¾ yd (4.4 m) of backing fabric

RIGHT The quilt is large enough to cover the top of a double bed and hang neatly over the sides. A variation of the central motif forms a pretty border at the edges.

- Batting to fit
- Monofilament thread
- White sewing thread to match background fabric
- 3¾ yd (3.5 m) of freezer paper
- Large adhesive stick
- Template plastic
- Blu-Tack and an ¾ inch (18 mm) coin (e.g. a dime)

- Liquid Pins or No More Pins
- ¼ in (6 mm) quilters press bar
- 28, 17 and 15 in (71, 43 and 38 cm) squares of white paper
- Dark marking pen
- Rotary cutter, ruler and mat
- Open-toed embroidery foot
- Continuous leaf pattern stencil

The Rose of Sharon pieces are appliquéd onto white print background fabric. Thirteen diamond-shaped main blocks are arranged to form a central square. Two triangular blocks occupy each side edge, and a slightly smaller block the same shape fills each corner. The result is a perfectly symmetrical design.

APPLIQUE PREPARATION

1 Trace the appliqué shapes on sheet B of the fold out sheets in the center of this book onto template plastic and cut out carefully. Trace around the templates onto the dull side of freezer paper, using a sharp pencil. A total of 332 leaves, seventy-seven red flowers, thirteen large pink flowers and sixty-eight calyxes need to be traced. A small dab of Blu-Tack will help hold the templates in place while tracing. Use a ¾ inch (18 mm) coin as a template for the seventy-seven small circles for the yellow centers of the red flowers. Hold the coin in place with Blu-Tack. The pink buds are folded squares of fabric, so a template is not used for these. Cut out all the shapes carefully.

CUTTING THE FABRIC

2 From the background fabric, cut a length of 2⅞ yd (2.6 m) and fold in half lengthwise. Remove the selvage edges and cut 6 x 17 in (15 x 43 cm) squares at the selvage edge, which will yield a total of twelve squares for the main blocks. Another 17 in (43 cm) square will be cut in the next stage. From the folded edge of the fabric, cut eighteen 16½ x 2½ in (420 x 63 mm) lengths for short sashing strips.

3 Cut the remainder of the folded fabric into 2½ in (63 mm) wide strips for long sashing pieces, again cutting along the length of the fabric. Cut another length of background fabric 59 in (1.5 meters). Without folding the fabric, cut two 28 in (71 cm) squares from one side selvage edge after removing this selvage. These are reserved for the setting triangles. From the other side of the fabric edge, cut a 17 in (43 cm) square to make a total of thirteen main blocks. Also cut two 15½ in (39 cm) squares for the corner setting triangles. From the remaining 35½ in (90 cm) background fabric, cut eight strips 2¼ in (57 mm) wide and reserve for the binding. Also cut six strips 2½ in (63 mm) wide for the long sashing strips. These strips should all be cut from selvage to selvage.

4 Cut the green print fabric into four lengths: Two 19⅝ in (50 cm) pieces, one 9⅞ in (25 cm) piece and one 4 in (10 cm) piece. Bias strips will be cut from these pieces. (Making strips from these lengths is easier than making them from the full 1½ yd/1.35 m piece of fabric.)

5 From the first 19⅝ in (50 cm) length, cut fourteen bias strips 1⅛ in (29 mm) wide, cutting the fabric from the lower left-hand corner to the top at a 45 degree angle. From the second 19⅝ in (50 cm) length of fabric, cut another five bias strips 1⅛ in (29 mm) wide in the same manner. From the 9⅞ in (25 cm) length, cut thirteen strips 1⅛ in (29 mm) wide. The remainder of the green print fabric from the above three pieces and also the extra 10 cm of green fabric are used to cut out the leaves and calyxes.

6 Cut three strips of pink fabric 1½ in (38 mm) wide, across the width of the fabric. Crosscut these strips into sixty-eight 1½ in (38 mm) squares.

MAKING THE BIAS STEMS

7 Stitch the bias lengths together, along the long edge with wrong sides together, using ¼ in (6 mm) seam allowance. Trim the seam allowance to approximately ⅛ in (3 mm). Insert the ¼ in (6 mm) press bar into the tube and roll the seam to the center of the flat side of the bar. Press the seam allowance in one direction, slipping the bar through the tubes of fabric as they are pressed.

8 The bias strips made from 19⅝ in (50 cm) lengths of green fabric are used on the main blocks and the shorter strips are used for the setting and corner triangles. Run a thin line of Liquid Pins down the center of the seam allowance when the bias strips are ready to be positioned. This will hold the bias strips in place when blind hem stitching. If the Liquid Pins is not dry when you are ready to stitch, apply the heat from a hair dryer to the wrong side of the background square.

Green print fabric

14 strips 1⅛ in wide

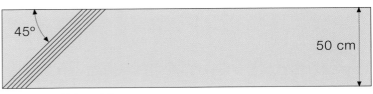

5 strips 1⅛ in wide

13 strips 1⅛ in wide

Remaining green fabric

BLIND HEM APPLIQUEING

9 Press the prepared freezer paper appliqué shapes to the wrong side of the chosen fabrics, with the shiny side against the fabric. Leave about ½ in (13 mm) between each shape.

10 Cut out the pieces carefully, adding ³⁄₁₆ in (5 mm) seam allowance around each of the pieces. Run an adhesive stick around the edge of the freezer paper shapes and carefully finger press the fabric seam allowance under.

11 Clip only the inner curves of the appliqué pieces. Make tiny gathers to create a smooth outer curve. Use a seam ripper or tailor's awl to hold these gathers in place as you glue them.

12 Place monofilament thread on the top of the machine and regular sewing thread in the bobbin. Select the blind hem stitch function on the machine, and set the stitch width position to 1.0 and the stitch length to 0.5. If the machine does not have a blind hem stitch function, use a very open (long stitch length) and narrow (stitch width) zigzag stitch. The left swing of the needle should catch the edge of the appliqué piece and the straight stitch should be just off the edge and sewn on the background fabric. It may be necessary to reduce the top tension to prevent the bobbin thread showing on the top of the work. Use an open-toed embroidery/appliqué foot for better visibility.

13 After you have stitched the appliqué piece, cut the background fabric away from behind, leaving a seam allowance of ¼ in (6 mm). Spray the exposed freezer paper with water to dissolve the adhesive. Leave for 5 to 10 minutes, then carefully pull away the paper, supporting the blind hem stitching line at the same time. (Note: You must remove the paper from behind the pink flowers before stitching the red flowers in place, and you must remove the paper from behind the red flowers in the same manner before stitching the yellow centers.)

MAKING THE MAIN APPLIQUE BLOCKS

14 With a dark marking pen, trace the quarter block (see sheet B of the fold-out sheets in the back of this book) onto a 17 in (43 cm) square of white paper. Using the marked center lines, keep moving the quarter block clockwise until you have drawn the full block onto the paper.

15 Fold the 17 in (43 cm) square of background fabric into quarters and press lightly. Pin the background fabric to the paper pattern using the center lines to line up the pattern correctly.

16 Lightly trace the appliqué pieces to the background fabric, keeping the pencil lines within the appliqué shapes. Only draw a thin line down the center of the bias stems as a placement guide.

17 Following the directions for bias stems, glue these in place with Liquid Pins, and then pin the leaves and main flowers in place. Before pinning the calyxes in place, fold the 1½ in (38 mm) pink squares in half diagonally and then bring both the outer points down to the lower point of the triangle and press carefully. The bud is then pinned in place underneath the calyx. Any excess folds of pink fabric are trimmed away from under the calyx when the calyx freezer paper is removed.

18 Stitch all pieces (apart from the buds which are only caught down under the calyxes) using the blind hem stitch method.

19 Remove the freezer paper as described previously, then stitch the red center flower in place. After removing the paper from behind the red center flower, stitch all the yellow centers in place, repeating this process to remove paper from behind them. Make thirteen main blocks in this way and then carefully trim each of the blocks back to a 16½ in (42 cm) square.

FORMING THE SIDE SETTING TRIANGLES

20 Rule two diagonal lines through a 28 in (71 cm) square of paper and, using the same method as in the main blocks, trace the side setting in each quarter of the square. Fold the 28 in (71 cm) square of background fabric in half diagonally and then in half again on the other diagonal. Press lightly.

21 Trace the pattern lightly onto each of the four quarters of the background fabric and, using the same method as the main blocks, appliqué the pieces in place. Repeat the procedure described above for the other 28 in (71 cm) square of background fabric. Each square is then cut into four triangles using the pressing lines as guides. These triangles will be slightly larger than required. They will be trimmed after the quilt top is assembled and sewn together.

FORMING THE CORNER SETTING TRIANGLES

22 Rule one diagonal line through a 15½ in (39 cm) square of paper and trace the corner setting triangle onto either side of the line, using the leaves indicated by the dotted lines on the pattern. Note that the bias stem ends under a leaf on either side and that the lower leaves are also in a slightly different position to those of the side setting triangles. Appliqué the pieces in place, then cut square on the diagonal line to form two triangles. Repeat this procedure for the other square.

ASSEMBLING THE QUILT TOP

23 Referring to the Layout diagram below, stitch the 16½ x 2½ in (420 x 63 mm) strips to join the blocks together to form diagonal rows. Press the seams towards the sashing strips. Then add side setting triangles to the ends of the appropriate rows. Note those sides of the triangles that have bias edges and take care not to stretch these sides.

Layout

24 Join the remaining 2½ in (63 mm) strips together with 45 degree angles to form one long strip. Lay the diagonal quilt rows out on the floor and check that the measurements of the quilt top rows match those on the Layout diagram.

25 Cut the sashing strips to the required lengths. Add these long sashing strips to the sides of the rows and pin in place to join the quilt top together. Pin carefully making sure that the quilt blocks remain aligned on either side of the sashing strip.

Key
a = Short sashing strips
b = Long sashing strips
c = Side setting triangles
d = Corner setting triangles

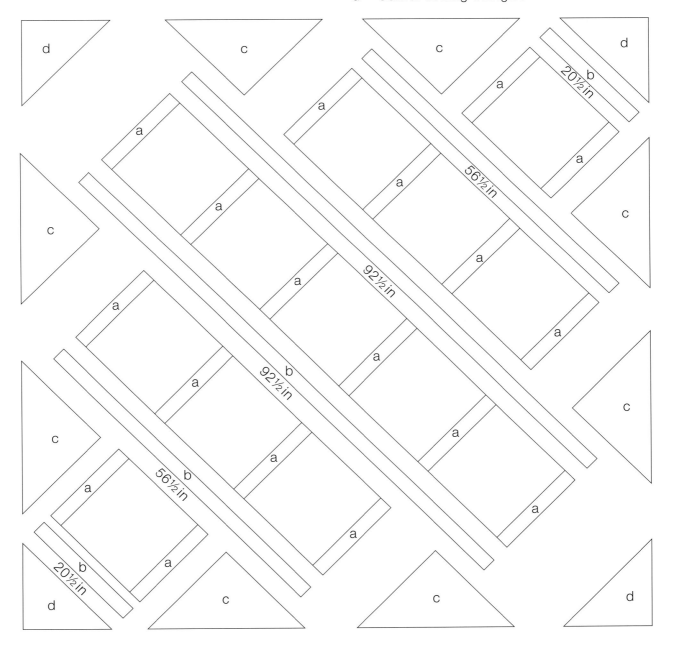

26 Sew the pieces together and press all seams towards the sashing strips. Then sew the corner setting triangles in place, again taking care that the bias edge is not stretched.

27 Press seams towards the sashing strips. Trim the quilt top. A large carpenter's set square is handy if available. Note that the setting triangles extend ¼ in (6 mm) beyond the edges of the sashing strips.

QUILTING

28 Mark any necessary quilting lines on the top of the quilt. Outline quilt around the appliquéd shapes, then stitch in-the-ditch around each of the quilt blocks.

29 Stitch the sashing strips using a continuous leaf pattern. (A stencil of this pattern can be obtained at sewing shops.)

BINDING

30 Join the eight 2¼ in (57 mm) wide strips with 45 degree angles to make one long strip, and press the seams open. Press the length of binding in half, wrong sides together.

31 Using a ¼ in (6 mm) seam, stitch the binding around the edge of the quilt, with all raw edges even and mitring each corner.

32 Trim the excess batting and backing fabric to approximately ¼ in (6 mm) beyond the edge of the quilt top. Roll the binding to the back of the quilt and hand stitch in place. Attach a label to the back of the quilt.

QUILTS IN THE COLONIES

North America

Before it won independence from Britain, the United States imported all its goods and fabric was scarce and expensive. Women used whatever they had to quilt bedding, and old quilts, corn husks and grasses often served as batting. Because most women did not have the luxury of being able to use large pieces of fabric for the quilt design, they devised simple blocks that used small pieces of triangular and square fabric instead and placed the blocks together or separated them with sashings to form different patterns. Designs featuring the four- and nine-patch block, made from four or nine squares, were popular because they were simple and could be sewn quickly.

For women migrating westwards with their families seeking new farmland, quilts were very important. They not only provided bedding but also connected them to their homelands and to their now distant friends, and could be used for wrapping fragile objects such as china, for padding a seat and for covering those who died on the journey for burial. A quilt made while travelling often reflected the journey. The Road to California design is an example of this. Other blocks recalled the literature that women read on the way (the Lady of the Lake block is one example) and the homes they left behind (the inspiration for the Fox and Geese design). All of these designs involved the manipulation of squares and triangles.

Once settled, women began to make quilts which reflected their new surroundings and homes (the Autumn Leaves and the Log Cabin block are two examples). The Log Cabin block was especially popular, as it required only small, thin scraps of fabric, and if sewn onto a foundation fabric, when finished needed no quilting. In addition to this, the block's design, with its two light and two dark sides, permitted many variations, and was hardwearing. The center of the block was traditionally either red or yellow. The use of this single central color lent unity to the design regardless of the number of different fabrics used for the logs. Red signified a warm fire in the hearth, and yellow a lighted candle in the window, placed there at night to guide menfolk home.

The local church was the center of social as well as religious life for farming communities. To help a fellow parishioner with a farm project, the congregation would gather and while the men worked, the women would sit around a frame and quilt. These gatherings, which became known as 'quilting bees', were a forum for sharing quilting ideas and patterns.

The Fox and Geese design was popular with early American pioneers; it represented the homes they left behind.

Religious themes were often used for quilts. The Rose of Sharon pattern is an example of such a design. The flower depicted is mentioned in the Bible's Song of Solomon. Chapter 2, Verse 1 begins with the words 'I am the rose of Sharon, and the lily of the valleys'.

Quilting also has a long tradition in other former British colonies, such as Australia. Crazy patch quilts, embroidered with rich silks, satins and velvets came into vogue towards the close of the 19th century. During the Great Depression of the 1930s, the scrap quilt became popular once again. Old pieces of men's suiting and women's clothing were used to cover and line cereal sacks, creating a type of sleeping bag often known as a 'wagga'.

Other quilts of the time are recognisable for their vibrant, cheerful colors, bright red in particular, and nostalgic designs: Grandmother's Fan, Dresden Plate and Grandmother's Flower Garden were much favored.

A Walk through the Forest

To create this superb quilt inspired by the forest floor, gather all the green, beige, brown and purple fabrics in your collection. Then go for a stroll in the woods or the country for inspiration and absorb the sights of nature. Look at the exquisite tiny flowers and unusual twigs and at the patterns caused by sunlight shining through the branches of trees. Transform the experience into this beautiful crazy patch quilt.

Finished size For a wall or a throw (175 x 140 cm; 69 x 55 in)

Unlike traditional quilt blocks, which are pieced with pure cotton fabrics, crazy patch blocks are made of fabrics of all persuasions—velvets, satins and silks as well as cottons are used in this block.

LEFT Bring the outdoors into your home with this forest theme crazy patch quilt. Made to be admired, it features lavish embroidered blocks.

Materials

◆ A collection of different fabrics suitable for your design, or ¼ yd (20 cm) of fifteen to twenty different fabrics
◆ 1½ yd (1.4 m) of foundation fabric
◆ 2 yd (1.8 m) each of lattice strips, borders and binding
◆ 3¼ yd (2.8 m) of backing fabric
◆ 2¼ yd x 54 in (2 x 1.5 m) of wadding

CUTTING THE FABRIC

1 Cut the foundation fabric into twenty 11 in (28 cm) squares. Then cut four 4½ in x 2 yd (115 mm x 1.8 m) strips from the border fabric .

2 Cut fifteen lattice strips of 2½ x 10½ in (63 mm x 27 cm) and then cut four more strips of 2½ x 46½ in (63 mm x 118 cm) from the same fabric. Cut four 2¾ in x 2 yd (70 mm x 1.8 meter) strips of the same fabric for the binding.

MAKING THE BLOCKS

Note: Trim each seam back to ¼ in (6 mm) as you work and press after making each seam.

3 Cut a five-sided piece of fabric and position it within the center of the foundation fabric. Sew a piece of fabric, wrong sides together, to one side of the five-sided piece then sew pieces of fabric to the remaining sides, working in a clockwise direction. Use different fabrics for each of the pieces and press the pieces and trim the seams back to ¼ in (6 mm) as you go.

Sewing a fabric piece to a five-sided piece

4 Continue to cover the foundation block, using different fabrics to create the look you want. Make sure that each piece extends beyond the piece you attach it to. You may find that a fabric piece is not large enough to cover the previous piece. If this happens, there are several things that you can do:
■ You can fold a seam under and press and sew on the other side and anchor this open seam with embroidery.
■ You can sew several small pieces together to create a long piece, then sew this to the foundation unit.
■ You can appliqué curves, triangles or squares on top to hide a raw edge or to extend a seam to fit.

Extending a piece beyond a previous piece

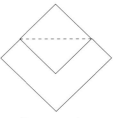

Press under

Long piece

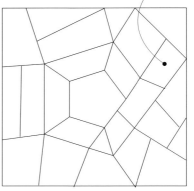

Curved piece

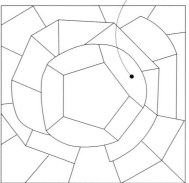

Forming the foundation block

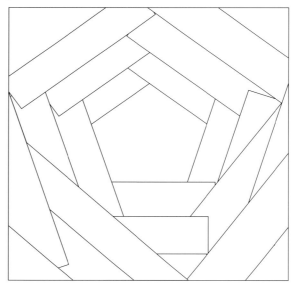

Beige, green and purple are used with dramatic results in this quilt. The effect is heightened by the thick, brightly colored embroidery stitches anchoring the block pieces.

5 When you have completed sewing all the blocks, embroider them using a sewing machine or by hand. You could follow the theme of the forest floor and embroider leaves and pathways or you could embroider motifs of your own choice.

6 Cut the finished blocks back to 10½ in (27 cm), then sew ⅛ in (3 mm) around the edge of all of the blocks in order to secure them.

7 Lay the blocks out, four across and five down, with an even balance of color. Sew a 2½ x 10½ in (63 mm x 27 cm) strip between each block, across the width of the quilt.

Laying out the strips

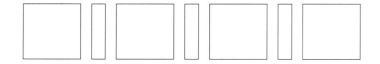

8 Sew the 2½ x 46½ in (63 mm x 118 cm) strips to each of the rows of blocks.

Sewing the 2½ x 46½ in strips

9 Lay the backing down, wrong side up, and place the wadding on top of it, leaving 2 in (50 mm) around the edge. Place the quilt top down, right side up, and, using safety pins, pin it firmly to the wadding and backing layers below.

10 Machine or hand quilt the top. For this quilt, the blocks were anchored and then the lattice strips and borders were machine quilted with leaves, in keeping with the forest floor theme.

Sewing the borders

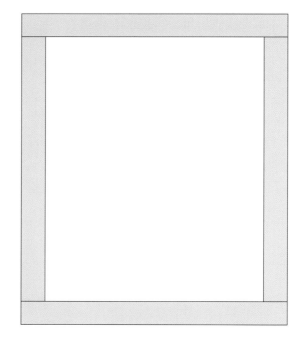

Embroidered leaves and pathways

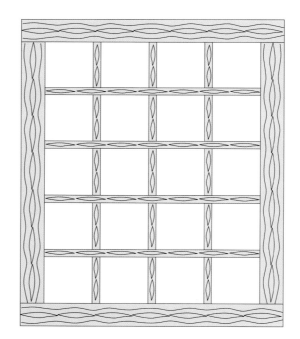

11 Fold the binding fabric wrong sides together and press. Align the raw edges together and sew a ¼ in (6 mm) seam allowance from the edge. Sew the two sides first, then the top and the bottom. Cut the wadding and backing to ½ in (13 mm) from the stitching line. Press and fold over to the back of the quilt and slip stitch in place.

CARING FOR AND STORING QUILTS

Conserving quilts

Quilts are affected by dirt, chemicals, light, heat, humidity and pests. The following measures should be adopted to remove these harmful agents from a quilt's environment.

■ As soon as a quilt is finished, it should be washed thoroughly in tepid water to remove any grit, grime and chemicals that accumulated while it was being made.

■ All forms of light are damaging to quilts, but particularly ultraviolet light—that is, sunlight and fluorescent light. The damage caused by this light is cumulative and irreversible. Ultraviolet light breaks down dyes and makes fabric fibres brittle. Incandescent light (tungsten), while not ultraviolet and as damaging as fluorescent light, gives off heat, which causes fabric fibres to degrade. To diminish the harmful effects of light, quilts should be kept out of the path of direct sunlight and reflected glare and UV filters should be placed on fluorescent lights or indirect, incandescent light used instead.

■ The air around a quilt should be neither too wet nor too dry: Fifty per cent relative humidity is ideal. High humidity causes dyes to fade rapidly and encourages moulds, bacteria and water staining. Very dry conditions can cause fabric fibres to become brittle or cracked. Good air circulation is needed to maintain a safe environment. Windows should be left open when weather permits. Alternatively, fans can be used to circulate air. A wet quilt should be dried quickly (within a couple of hours). A fan may be used to do this or the quilt placed outdoors on a clean, dry surface out of direct sunlight.

■ Rodents and insect pests are attracted to dark, warm, undisturbed places, such as cupboards used as storage areas for quilts. Quilts stored in cupboards should be checked regularly for signs of pest damage. Careful vacuuming will remove eggs, larvae and cocoons as well as dead insects. Moth crystals are recommended to discourage pests of this type. Place the quilt in two layers of polyethelene bags with a packet of para-dichlorobenzene crystals wrapped in acid-free tissue paper.

Cleaning and storing quilts

A quilt should be aired periodically to stop it getting musty. Shake out the dust and hang it in a breezy spot in the shade. If a quilt is very dirty, the best and safest method of cleaning it is to gently vacuum it from the wrong side, using the brush attachment on the vacuum cleaner.

Ideally, quilts should be stored unstacked, that is flat and unfolded. The best way to do this is to place a quilt on or under a bed. It is generally more convenient to store quilts in a cupboard. To avoid exposing quilts to adverse conditions, make sure the cupboard is cool and its back faces the light. Don't crowd the cupboard, so that air is able to circulate around the quilts. If there is room, roll each quilt around a fabric tube and tie with ribbon to prevent permanent creases developing. Quilts that are stored folded should be refolded periodically.

To avoid creases developing, stored quilts should be rolled around fabric tubes.

Houses in
the Cabins

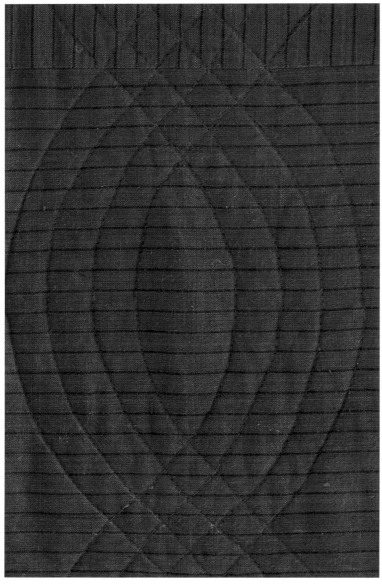

The deep blue second border of the quilt top is quilted using a cable pattern.

In this clever variation of the traditional Log Cabin pattern, Log Cabin blocks, made from light- and dark-colored fabric, frame five feature blocks representing houses. The result is a contemporary design imbued with an old-world charm.

Finished size For a queen-size bed (234 x 274 cm; 92 x 108 in)

RIGHT The Log Cabin block, a symbol of the American frontier, owes much of its popularity to its versatility—it is able to accommodate many design variations.

Materials

- ⅝ yd (50 cm) of yellow fabric for centers and windows
- ½ yd (40 cm) of first border fabric
- 2¾ yd (2.5 m) of second border fabric
- 8¼ yd(7.5 m) of backing fabric
- 2¾ yd (2.5 m) of continuous wadding 3¼ yd (3 m) wide, or queen-size batting
- ⅞ yd (75 cm) of binding

Light (cream) check fabric

- ⅔ yd (60 cm) of four different white or white blend fabrics for the Log Cabin blocks
- 1 yd (90 cm) of four different very light fabrics for the Log Cabin blocks
- ¼ yd (20 cm) each of five different white or white blend fabrics or very light fabrics for the house blocks
- 1⅓ yd (1.2 m) of four different light fabrics
- 2½ yd (2.2 m) of five different medium light fabrics

Dark (blue) check fabric

- ⅝ yd (50 cm) of six different light fabrics
- ⅞ yd (75 cm) of six different medium fabrics
- 1⅛ yd (1 m) of six different medium dark fabrics
- 2 yd (1.75 mm) of six different dark fabrics

Medium (red) check fabric

- Fat ⅛ of five different light fabrics
- Fat ⅛ of five different medium fabrics
- Fat ¼ of two different dark fabrics

CUTTING THE FABRIC

Note: Cut all fabric selvage to selvage.

1 From the yellow fabric, cut five 2 in (50 mm) strips for the Log Cabin block centers. Crosscut into ten 2 in (50 mm) lengths.

2 Select the light (cream) check fabrics. Cut eighteen 1¼ in (32 mm) strips from the white/white blends and twenty-six 1¼ in (32 mm) strips from the very light fabrics. Also cut thirty-five 1¼ in (32 mm) strips from the light fabrics and forty-six 1¼ in (32 mm) strips from the medium light fabrics.

3 Select the dark (blue) check fabric, cut fourteen 1¼ in (32 mm) strips from the light fabrics, twenty-two 1¼ in (32 mm) strips from the medium fabrics, thirty-one 1¼ in (32 mm) strips from the medium dark fabrics and thirty-eight 1¼ in (32 mm) strips from the dark fabrics.

4 For the house block windows, cut two 2½ in (63 mm) strips from the yellow fabric. Crosscut the strips into ten 2½ x 5 in (63 x 127 mm) rectangles.

5 For the house block background, for each of the five blocks, from the white/white blends fabric, cut one 2½ in (62 mm) strip. Recut into a 2½ x 4 in (63 x 100 mm) rectangle (part i), a 2½ x 3 in (63 x 76 mm) rectangle (part iii) and a 2½ x 6½ in (63 x 165 mm) rectangle (part ii). Cut the shape of the part iv Corner Sky Template, the part vi Corner Sky Template and the Sky Template (part v) (see sheet D of the fold-out sheets in the back of this book). Cut a 1½ in (38 mm) strip. Recut into a 1½ x 15½ in (38 x 394 mm) length (part vii) and a 1½ x 8½ in (38 x 216 mm) rectangle (part viii).

6 Select the medium (red) check fabrics. For each of the five house blocks, from the light fabrics, cut a shape using the Gable Template, two 2 x 7 in (50 x 178 mm) rectangles (part a) and a 2 x 5½ in (50 x 140 mm) rectangle (part b). From the second light fabric, cut two 2 x 2½ in (50 x 63 mm) lengths for the chimneys. From the medium light fabrics, cut two 2 x 5 in (50 x 127 mm) rectangles (part x), a 2½ x 5 in (63 x 127 mm) rectangle (part y), a 2 x 9½ in (50 x 240 mm) rectangle (part w) and a 2½ x 9½ in (63 x 240 mm) rectangle (part z). From the dark fabrics, using the Roof Template, cut a piece for the roof.

7 From the dark (blue) checks, cut one 2½ x 7 in (63 x 178 mm) rectangle for the door of the house for each of the five house blocks.

8 From the first border fabric, cut nine 1½ in (38 mm) strips. Join the strips together to make one continuous length. Recut into two 1½ x 77½ in (38 mm x 197 cm) lengths for the top and bottom border and two 1½ x 90½ (38 mm x 230 cm) in lengths for the side borders.

9 From the second border fabric, cut four 8 x 92½ in (203 mm x 235 cm) lengths down the fabric (parallel to the selvage).

10 For the backing, cut fabric into three 2¾ yd (2½ meter) lengths. Join the lengths together down the selvage to make a 2¾ x (approximately) 3½ yd (2½ x 3.3 meter) length. Cut the 3½ yd (3.3 meter) length down to a length of approximately 3⅕ yd (2.9 meter) length. (Use the remaining 15¾ in x 2¾ yd (40 cm x 2.5 meter) piece for the rod pocket at the back of the quilt.)

11 For the binding, cut eleven 2¼ in (57 mm) strips. Join the strips together with a bias seam to make one continuous length.

The 'Barn Raising' Log Cabin pattern, in which the light and dark strips in the Log Cabin blocks are arranged to create diamond shapes, is used to great effect in this quilt. The red fabric strips in the house blocks and the bright yellow centers of the log blocks add warmth.

MAKING THE LOG CABIN BLOCKS

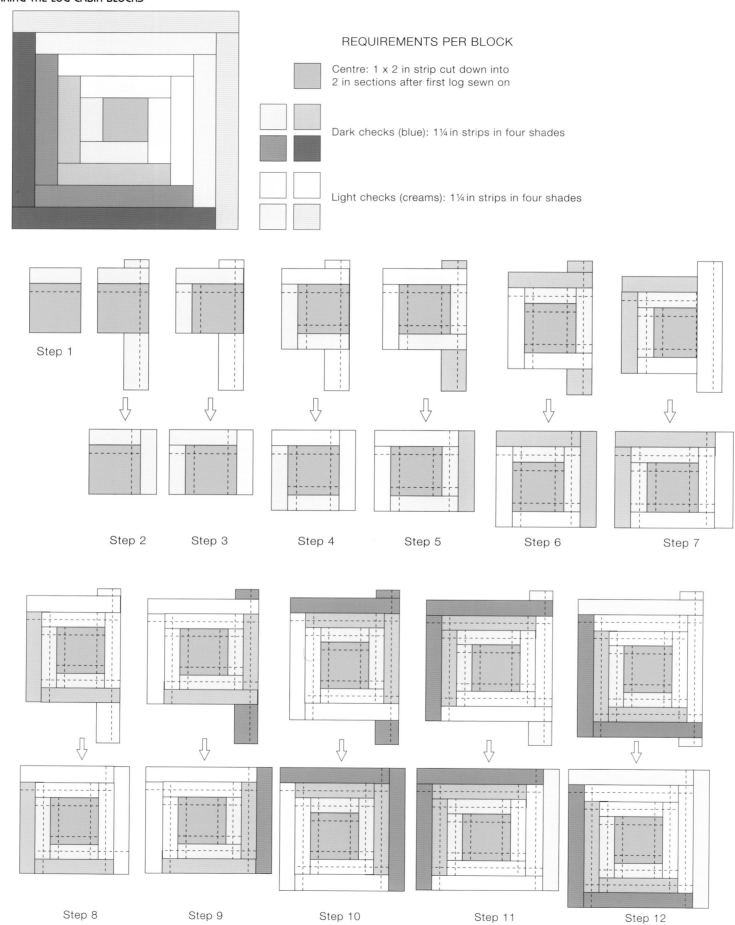

REQUIREMENTS PER BLOCK

Centre: 1 x 2 in strip cut down into
2 in sections after first log sewn on

Dark checks (blue): 1¼ in strips in four shades

Light checks (creams): 1¼ in strips in four shades

Step 1

Step 2   Step 3   Step 4   Step 5   Step 6   Step 7

Step 8   Step 9   Step 10   Step 11   Step 12

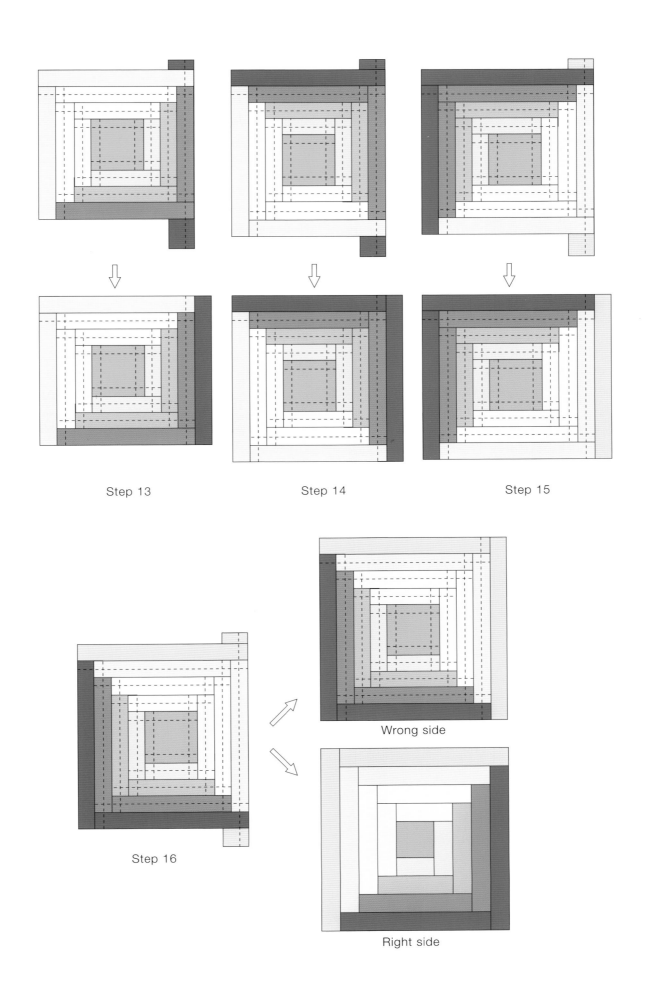

Step 13

Step 14

Step 15

Step 16

Wrong side

Right side

MAKING THE LOG CABIN BLOCKS

12 When making the log cabin blocks, bear these points in mind:

■ The log just sewn should go to the top and the new strip should lie next to the machine's feed dogs, to be used as a straight edge guide.

■ Make 100 blocks.

■ To provide variety, spread the fabrics used for the logs around. For example, if you begin with ten blocks that have the same first dark check logs, use different light check logs.

■ Alternate the order of the fabrics on both the light and the dark sides of the block. You may find that you end up with a couple of blocks that have the same fabric, but generally the order of the fabrics should appear to be random. The more fabrics you have for the blocks, the greater variety you will be able to achieve.

■ The log cabin blocks around the house blocks should have very light, light check sides so that the house blocks appear to 'float' on the background and don't have obvious boundaries. You will need forty log cabin blocks with very light sides to go around the house blocks.

13 Sew a 2 in (50 mm) yellow center strip, down the length, to a 1¼ in (32 mm) light dark check strip. Iron away from the center towards the dark check. Using a rotary cutter and ruler, cut the strip into 10 x 2 in (254 x 50 mm) pieces.

14 Take a diagram step 1 unit (see page 44) and, using the same light dark (blue) check fabric, sew a strip to the unit to form a diagram step 2 unit. Iron away from the center. Using the rotary cutter and the ruler, trim the block to size.

15 Sew the step 2 unit to a light white/white blend check strip (see page 44). Iron away from the center. Using the rotary cutter and ruler, trim the block to size.

16 Sew the same light white/white blend check strip to the diagram step 3 unit (see page 44). Iron away the from center. Using the rotary cutter and ruler, trim the block to size.

17 Sew a medium dark check strip to the diagram step 4 unit (see page 44). Iron away from the center. Using the rotary cutter and ruler, trim the block to size.

18 Sew the same medium dark check strip to the diagram step 5 unit (see page 44). Iron away from the center. Using the rotary cutter and ruler, trim the block to size.

19 Sew the diagram step 6 unit to a light, light check strip

(see page 44) to create a diagram step 7 unit. Iron away from the the center. Using the rotary cutter and ruler, trim the block to size.

20 Follow the diagrams on pages 44 and 45 to sew the step 8 to step 16 units. The step 16 unit should have four shades of light check on one side of the block and four shades of dark check on the other side of the block. The same fabric will be used twice, to do two logs, on each block. For each log, iron away from the center of the block and use the rotary cutter and ruler to trim the block.

MAKING THE HOUSE BLOCKS

21 To form the chimney section, referring to the diagram on page 47, sew a background piece (i) to a chimney rectangle, to a background piece (ii), to the second chimney rectangle, to a background piece (iii). Iron in the direction of the arrows.

22 To form the roof/gable section, using the templates you have cut from sheet D of the fold-out sheets in the center of this book, cut out templates for the gable, roof and background pieces ((iv), (v) and (vi)) from template plastic. Then, using the plastic templates, cut the shapes from fabric, making sure that you cut all the templates from the right-side of the fabric. Sew the gable section to the background piece (v), making sure that you overlap the ends so that the ¼ in (6 mm) sewing line will run on where the two pieces overlap. Sew the roof piece onto the background piece (v), once again making sure that the ¼ in (6 mm) sewing line will run on where the two sections overlap. Sew the background triangle (iv) to the gable. Sew the background triangle (vi) to the roof. Iron in the direction of the arrows.

23 To form the background section, sew the chimney section to the roof/gable section. Sew the background section (the 1½ x 15½ in/38 x 394 mm rectangle) to the bottom of the roof/gable section. Iron in the direction of the arrows.

24 To form the house front section, sew a light medium check 2 x 7 in (50 x 178 mm) rectangle (a) to both sides of a door rectangle. Sew a light medium check 2 x 5½ in (50 x 140 mm) rectangle (b) to the top of the door unit. Iron in the direction of the arrows.

25 To form the house side section, sew a medium medium check 2 x 5 in (50 x 127 mm) rectangle (x) to a 2½ x 5 in (63 x 127 mm) window rectangle, to a medium medium check 2½ x 5 in (63 x 127 mm) rectangle (y), to the second

house block

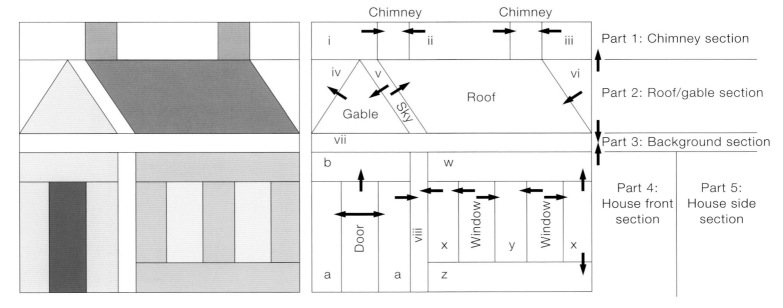

2½ x 5 in (63 x 127 mm) window rectangle, to the second medium medium check 2 x 5 in (50 x 127 mm) rectangle (x). Iron in the direction of the arrows. Sew a medium medium check 2 x 9½ in (50 mm x 24 cm) rectangle (w) to the top of the window section. Sew a medium medium check 2½ x 9½ in (63 mm x 24 cm) rectangle (z) to the bottom of the window section. Iron in the direction of the arrows.

26 Sew the house front section to the left-hand side of a background 1½ x 8½ in (38 mm x 22 cm) rectangle (viii). Sew the house side section to the right-hand side of the background 1½ x 8½ in (38 mm x 22 cm) rectangle (viii). Iron in the direction of the arrows. Make four more house blocks.

ASSEMBLING THE QUILT TOP

27 Follow the diagrams below and the diagrams and instructions on pages 48 and 49 to assemble the quilt top.

MAKING THE BORDERS

28 For the first border, sew the two 1½ x 90½ in (38 mm x 230 cm) lengths to each side of the quilt top. Iron towards the border.

29 Sew the two 1½ x 77½ in (38 mm x 197 cm) lengths to the top and the bottom of the quilt top. Again iron towards the border.

30 For the second border, sew two 8 x 92½ in (203 mm x 235 cm) lengths to each side of the quilt top. Iron towards the second border. Then sew the remaining two 8 x 92½ in (203 mm x 235 cm) lengths to the top and bottom of the quilt top. Again iron towards the second border.

31 Test a marking pen or pencil on a scrap of second border fabric before marking the entire quilt top. Using the Houses in the Cabin Second Border Quilting Pattern on sheet D of the fold-out sheets in the center of this book, mark the cable pattern in the second border.

32 Assemble the backing, batting and quilt top layers. Quilt in-the-ditch around all the blocks and borders. Then, for the house blocks, quilt in-the-ditch all the shapes in the house. Quilt the cables in the second border. Finally, quilt in-the-ditch using freehand quilting between the light and dark areas of each block, making sure that you quilt all sides of the center square of each block.

BINDING

33 When preparing the binding, it is a good idea to prepare a label and a sleeve for hanging the quilt (use the left-over piece of backing). These can be stitched with the binding or added when the binding is complete. Iron the continuous length in half, wrong sides together, down the entire length. With the raw edges of the binding matching the raw edges of the quilt, sew the binding to the quilt. Hand or machine stitch in place.

Assembling the quilt top

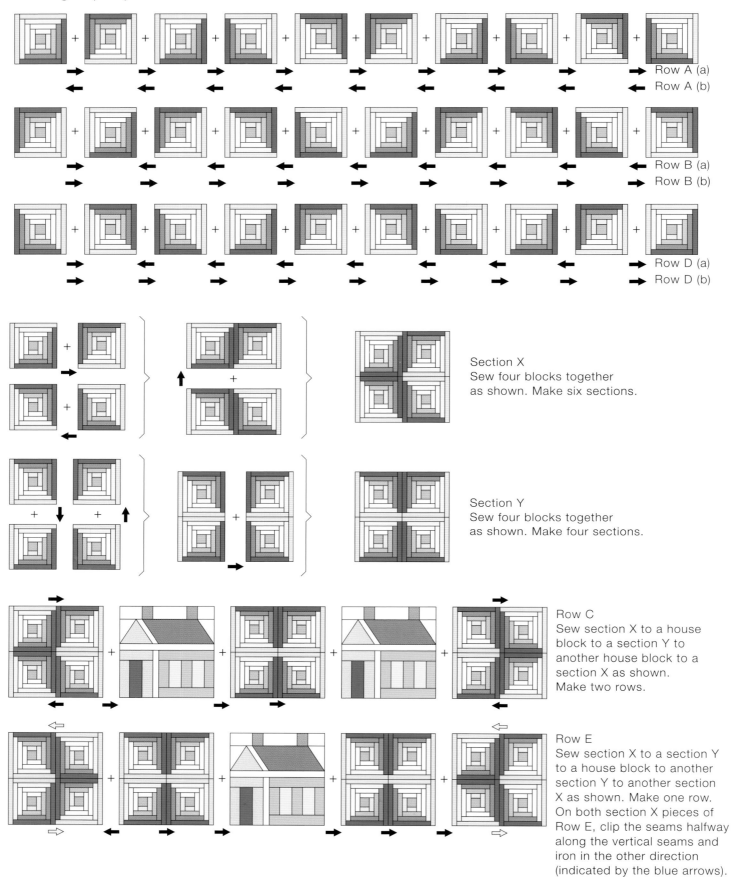

Row A (a)
Row A (b)

Row B (a)
Row B (b)

Row D (a)
Row D (b)

Section X
Sew four blocks together
as shown. Make six sections.

Section Y
Sew four blocks together
as shown. Make four sections.

Row C
Sew section X to a house
block to a section Y to
another house block to a
section X as shown.
Make two rows.

Row E
Sew section X to a section Y
to a house block to another
section Y to another section
X as shown. Make one row.
On both section X pieces of
Row E, clip the seams halfway
along the vertical seams and
iron in the other direction
(indicated by the blue arrows).

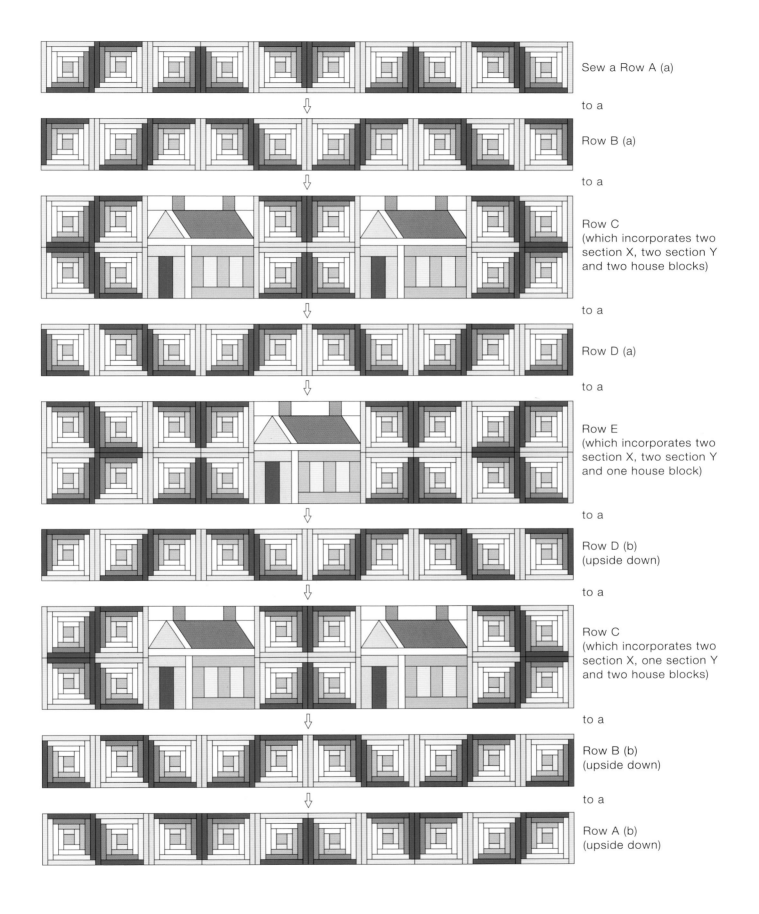

Sew a Row A (a)

⇩

to a

Row B (a)

⇩

to a

Row C
(which incorporates two
section X, two section Y
and two house blocks)

⇩

to a

Row D (a)

⇩

to a

Row E
(which incorporates two
section X, two section Y
and one house block)

⇩

to a

Row D (b)
(upside down)

⇩

to a

Row C
(which incorporates two
section X, one section Y
and two house blocks)

⇩

to a

Row B (b)
(upside down)

⇩

to a

Row A (b)
(upside down)

Lady of the Lake

Triangles of light and dark fabrics are arranged to represent the misty waters of the lady's lake.

The mysterious guardian of Excalibur in Arthurian legend is the inspiration for this quilt. Floral fabrics are used effectively throughout to give the sometimes sombre pattern a fresh, pretty look.

Finished size For a double bed (185 x 185 cm; 73 x 73 in)

Materials
- 13 x 7 in (33 x 18 cm) each of thirty-two light fabrics and thirty-two dark fabrics, for the small triangles (fabric A)
- ⅔ yd (60 cm) each of light and dark fabrics for the center of the blocks (fabric B)
- 1 yd (90 cm) of fabric for the triangles on the edge (fabric C)
- 2¼ yd (2 m) of fabric for borders (fabric D)
- ⅔ yd (60 cm) of binding fabric
- 4½ yd (4.1 m) of backing fabric
- 2¼ yd (2 m) square of wadding
- Rotary cutter, board and ruler

LEFT Dating from 1830, the Lady of the Lake block takes its name from the narrative poem by Sir Walter Scott. The pattern is of Amish origin.

- Iron and ironing surface
- Sewing machine
- Pins and general sewing supplies

MAKING THE QUILT TOP
1 Separate the thirty-two light and dark fabrics (fabric A) into pairs of complementary fabrics and place with right sides together. Draw a 3 in (76 mm) grid eight times.
2 Draw diagonal lines through the centers of the squares.

Grid

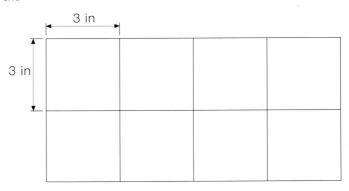

Drawing the diagonal lines

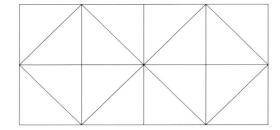

3 Pin the pieces.

Pinning

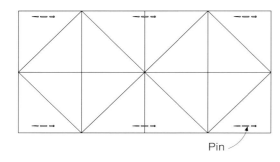

4 Sew along both sides of the diagonal lines, ¼ in (6 mm) from them.

Sewing

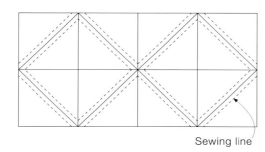

Sewing line

5 Cut through all the lines.

Cutting

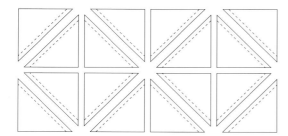

6 Press and trim back to 2½ in (63 mm).

Trimming

7 Using fabric B light and dark fabrics, draw a 7 in (18 cm) grid thirteen times. Repeat the procedure described in steps 3, 4, 5 and 6

8 Press and trim back to 6½ in (16.5 cm).

9 Arrange the block and sew the pieces together.

Arranging and sewing the block pieces

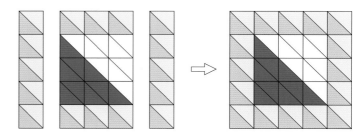

10 Using fabric C, cut three 15½ in (39 cm) squares and cut twice on the diagonal to make edge triangles.

Cutting on the diagonal

15½ in

8 in

11 Using fabric C, cut two 8 in (20 cm) squares and cut once on the diagonal to make corner triangles.

12 Arrange the blocks and triangles and sew diagonally across the quilt.

13 Cut borders the length of the fabric and 5 in (13 cm) wide. Sew the sides on, then the top and the bottom.

ASSEMBLING THE QUILT

14 Lay the backing down, then the wadding and place the quilt top on last. Clamp to a table, making sure that the quilt is smooth and firm, and pin for quilting.

QUILTING

15 Quilt in-the-ditch, cross-hatch the border and stipple the middle block.

BINDING

16 Cut the binding 2¾ in (70 mm), fold over, wrong sides together, and press. Place the raw edges together and stitch ¼ in (6 mm) from the edge.

17 Trim the backing and the wadding back to ½ in (13 mm) from the stitching line, then fold the binding to the back of the quilt, and, using slip stitch, sew it carefully in place.

Sewing the blocks and triangles

FABRIC FOR QUILTS

Preparing fabrics

Some quiltmakers think it a good idea to wash new fabrics before they begin making a quilt, to pre-shrink them and to ensure that they are colorfast. You can do this by setting the washing machine to wash fabrics in warm water, or by washing them by hand in the bath tub in tepid water. If a fabric bleeds while you are washing it, you can choose not to use it or you can set the dye yourself by adding cooking salt and/or vinegar to the water. Rinse the fabric, checking that the colors don't run. Iron the fabric while it is still damp.

Other quiltmakers prefer not to wash fabrics beforehand, as washing removes the protective coatings placed there by the manufacturers to discourage insects and to prevent the fabrics fading. The protective coating also keeps small strips of fabric from fraying.

Types of fabric

There are five main types of fabric. The first type of fabric is the solid. Solid fabrics are a uniform color and do not have a print or pattern.

The second type of fabric is the print. Prints are divided into three categories—small, medium and large. Small prints often look like solid fabrics from a distance. Medium prints are more distinct and are often used to add texture. Large prints are fabrics with very distinct patterns which stand out from their backgrounds, for example chintzes. Large prints are mainly used for borders in quilts.

The third type of fabric is the directional print. A directional print has a very distinct pattern that runs in one direction. If the print is small, a directional print can be used to form part of the quilt's design. Large, wide stripes can add elegance to a border.

The fourth type of fabric is the tone-on-tone. This is a print placed on a background in shades of the same color. Tone-on-tones come as small, medium or large prints and often appear to be solid fabrics from a distance. They are often used in a quilt to create tones of the same color.

Lastly, there is checked fabric. This is fabric with colored threads running at right angles to each other. Checks are popular for reproduction quilts.

Battings

The layer between the quilt top and the backing is called the batting. It is the part of the quilt that gives it its warmth. Polyester batts don't require much quilting and so are good for quilts used as wallhangings, for children's quilts and for quilts that are used all year round. Some polyester battings have a tendency to 'fight' the sewing machine. Wool batts are usually composed of blends of wool and polyester and provide more warmth and comfort than polyester batts. However, they require more quilting and those that are not needle-punched have a tendency to pill. Needle-punched wool and polyester blends are more stable and do not require as much quilting. Traditional cotton batts require a lot of quilting, some as much as every $\frac{1}{2}$ to 3 inches (13 to 76 mm). Needle-punched cotton batts are more stable and can be quilted up to 10 in (25 cm) apart. Generally, the most practical way to buy batting is on a roll as one continuous length; you can select the width that you need (battings generally come in widths of $2\frac{3}{8}$, $2\frac{5}{8}$ and $3\frac{1}{4}$ yards/2.2, 2.4 and 3 meters) and then buy the amount you require.

Labels

Labelling a quilt is a good way to establish a quilt's provenance and a satisfying way to advertize your clever handiwork. Information can be embroidered or cross-stitched directly onto the back of the quilt or can be handwritten, typed or printed in permanent ink on a piece of muslin and the muslin label sewn onto the quilt's backing fabric.

A label should include such information as the full names of the quiltmaker and the recipient, the type and the name of the quilt and when, where and how the quilt was made. The label should also give instructions on how to care for the quilt. Some quilters add a verse or message.

The most effective way to sew a label onto backing fabric is to 'quilt' the label in. Another way is to sew one side of the label into the binding and then to hand stitch the other three sides down after quilting.

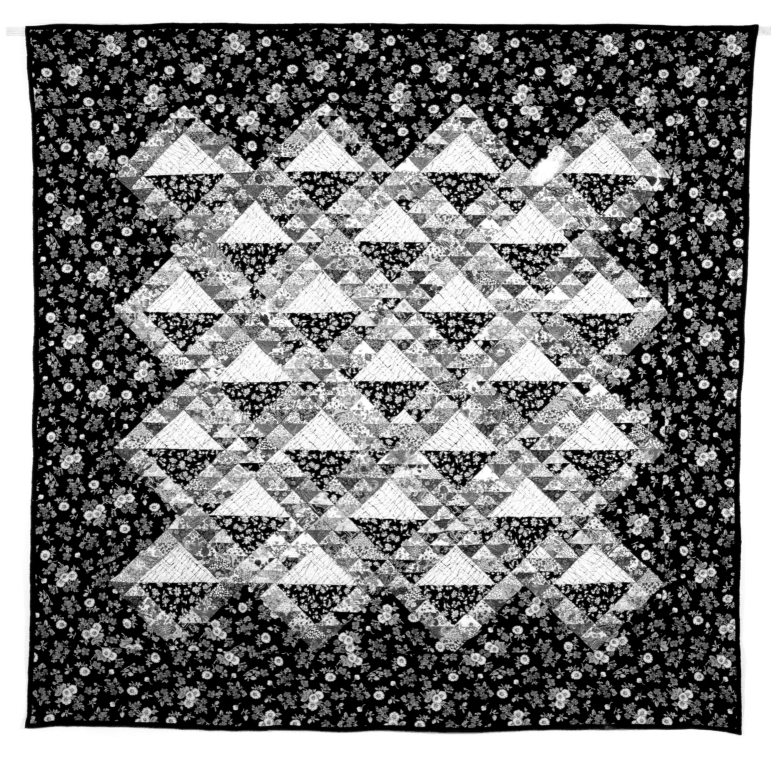

This is a large quilt designed to cover a double bed. A repeated block pattern of large and small triangles is the basis of the quilt's design. Light and dark fabrics in shades of blue create a tonal effect; the half-square triangles on the edges of the corner triangles appear to float on the fabric.

Autumn Leaves

Green and gold fall leaves are arranged around a central square of fabric.

This cosy quilt heralds the return of fall and cooler weather. The leaf blocks are constructed of half-square triangles and rectangular units. Cream fabric provides a crisp background for the leaf blocks. Borders in contrasting colors frame the design.

Finished size For a double bed (189 x 227 cm; 74½ x 89½ in)

Materials

- 139 in (3.5 m) of cream background fabric
- 15¾ in (40 cm) each of four green fabrics
- 15¾ in (40 cm) each of four gold fabrics
- 3⅞ in (10 cm) each of a green and gold contrast fabric
- 15¾ in (40 cm) of green fabric
- 86⅝ in (2.2 m) of printed fabric
- 196⅞ in (5 m) of backing fabric
- 82⅝ x 98⅜ in (2.1 x 2.5 m) of cotton wadding

RIGHT The large quilt makes a wonderful throw or a smart covering for a double bed. With its simple, contrasting color scheme, it is suitable for just about any interior.

- Two large reels of beige thread for piecing
- Green, cream and gold threads for quilting
- Rotary cutter, ruler and mat
- Sewing machine
- ¼ in (6 mm) sewing machine seam foot
- Safety pins

CUTTING THE FABRIC

1 From the cream background fabric, cut twelve strips 2⅞ in (73 mm) wide. From these crosscut 160, 2⅞ in (73 mm) squares. Cut these squares along one diagonal to create triangles for the blocks. From the same fabric, cut ten strips 2½ in (63 mm) wide. From these crosscut 160, 2½ in (63 mm) squares to use to piece the blocks. Then cut thirty-two strips 2 in (50 mm) wide. From these crosscut eighty lengths of 6½ in (165 mm) for the internal block sashings, and thirty-one lengths of 14 in (356 mm) for sashing between the blocks. The remaining eight strips are for the first border.

2 From each of the green and gold fabrics for the leaves, cut two strips 2⅞ in (73 mm) wide. From these, crosscut twenty 2⅞ in (73 mm) squares. Cut the squares along one diagonal to form triangles to use to piece the blocks. From each of the fabrics also cut three strips 2½ in (63 mm) wide. Crosscut into ten 4½ in (115 mm) lengths and twenty 2½ in (63 mm) squares.

3 From each of the green and gold contrast fabrics, cut a strip 2 in (50 mm) wide. From this crosscut ten 2 in (50 mm) squares for the middle of the blocks.

4 From the green border fabric, cut seven strips 1½ in (38 mm) wide for the inner border. From the printed fabric, cut a strip 2 in (50 mm) wide. From this crosscut twelve 2 in (50 mm) squares for the cornerstones in the sashing, nine strips 6 in (152 mm) wide for the outer border and ten strips 2¼ in (57 mm) wide for the binding.

CONSTRUCTING THE BLOCKS

5 Collect the 2⅞ in (73 mm) cream triangles and all green and gold 2⅞ in (73 mm) triangles. Stitch each cream triangle to a colored triangle along the bias edges. Press the seam away from the cream. Trim the corners.

6 Collect ten 2½ in (63 mm) squares from the green and gold leaf fabrics and eighty 2½ in (63 mm) squares of background fabric. Referring to the following diagram, make the stem of the leaves. Cut the cream background squares in half along one diagonal. Find the diagonal line

of the leaf fabric squares, then make cuts ½ in (13 mm) away from the diagonal on both sides to make the stem. Stitch a cream background triangle to either side of the leaf stem and press towards the stem.

Constructing a leaf stem

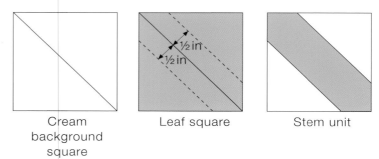

Cream background square   Leaf square   Stem unit

7 Each of the larger blocks is made of four smaller, individual leaf blocks. Make each leaf block in one fabric only. Take four triangle units made in Step 5, one stem made in Step 6, one cream 2½ in (63 mm) square, one 2½ in (63 mm) leaf square and a 2½ x 4½ in (63 x 115 mm) leaf rectangle. The leaf blocks can be broken up into three portions as shown in the diagram below. Stitch and press in the direction indicated by the arrows. Then stitch the three portions together to form the leaf. Make ten leaf blocks of each color, making a total of eighty.

Constructing a leaf block

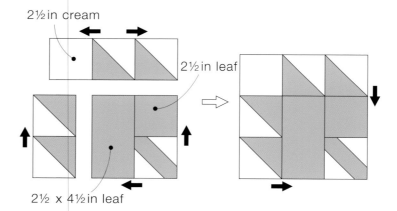

2½ in cream

2½ in leaf

2½ x 4½ in leaf

8 From the four green and four gold groups of leaves, select two green and two gold leaves for one block color unit. The remaining colors will make up the second color unit. For each block, place the two green leaves on the top left and bottom right corners and the gold leaves in the opposite two corners. The stems should all face inwards. Between the leaves place four 2 x 6½ in (50 x 165 mm) cream sashing strips and in the center place a 2 in contrast square. For one color unit use the green contrast and for the second unit use the gold contrast. Referring to the diagram, break the block up into three rows and

The cream background fabric is quilted using a diagonal pattern, creating a sense of movement. A cable pattern variation is used for the outer border.

stitch. Press all seams towards the sashing. Then sew the three rows together and press the seams towards the middle sashing. You should have ten blocks of each of the different color combinations.

Leaf blocks

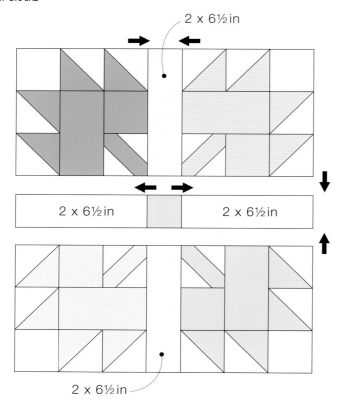

ASSEMBLING THE PIECES

9 The quilt is laid out in pieces by placing four large blocks across and five blocks down and putting sashings between these. Place the blocks down, alternating between the two-block color units and keeping the green leaves of all blocks in the top left-hand corner. This will result in all the green leaves being on one diagonal and all the gold being on the opposite diagonal.

10 Place the 2 x 14 in (50 x 355 mm) sashing strips between the blocks and the 2 in (50 mm) squares of the border fabric at the intersection of these sashings, as cornerstones.

11 Stitch the quilt together in rows of blocks and sashings, with alternating rows of sashings and cornerstones. Press all seams towards the sashings. When the rows are complete, stitch them together to form the center of the quilt. Again press towards the sashings.

12 The quilt's first border is a 2 in (50 mm) cream strip which floats above the leaf blocks. Measure across the quilt. Take the last eight 2 in (50 mm) wide strips of

cream. Join, using 45 degree seams, into four pairs of strips.

13 Cut two strips to the same measurement as the quilt and sew to the top and bottom of the quilt. Press the seam outwards. Measure the length of the quilt and cut the last two strips to equal the measurement of the quilt. Stitch to the sides of the quilt and again press outwards.

14 Repeat this process using the 1½ in (38 mm) wide green strips, and then repeat it with the 6 in (152 mm) wide printed outer border strips.

QUILTING

15 Cut two lengths of 2¾ yd (2.5 meters) of backing fabric. Join these together along the selvage edge of the fabric using a wide seam. Trim off the selvage and press the seam to one side.

16 Layer the backing fabric, batting and quilt top. Baste the three layers together with safety pins. With a sewing machine, stitch in-the-ditch along the main sashing strips to secure the pieces. Ditch stitch each leaf then echo quilt ¼ in (6 mm) in from the edge of the shape.

17 Quilt the cream background around each of the leaves using diagonal lines to create movement. Ditch stitch the seams between the borders. Quilt the outer border with a cable variation.

TO FINISH

18 Gather the ten 2¼ in (57 mm) strips of the printed fabric. Join these end to end to make one long strip, using 45 degree seams. Press the length of binding in half with wrong sides together. Using a ¼ in (6 mm) seam allowance, stitch the binding around the outer edge of the border. Keep all raw edges even and mitre the corners as you go.

19 Trim the excess batting and backing fabric back to approximately ¼ in (6 mm) past the edge of the border. Roll the binding to the back of the quilt and hand stitch in place.

TIPS FOR MAKING QUILTS

Work area

Creating a quilt is a lengthy process, so it is essential that you have a space in the home where you can work on, as well as leave, a quilt and necessary supplies.

Ideally, your workspace should be large enough to accommodate:
- a rotary cutting mat;
- a sewing table;
- an ironing board;
- cupboards for storing materials and supplies;
- a wall-mounted board for laying out your quilt designs.

To view your work adequately and to save your eyes, your workspace should be fitted with effective lighting. For viewing colored fabrics, color-corrected fluorescent overhead lights are essential. To sew, good task lighting is important— clamp on or free-standing lights are useful in this regard.

Foundation piecing

Follow these sewing tips to make foundation piecing a bit easier:
- When possible, stitch in the direction of points—this will make it easier for you to cross seam lines exactly.
- For better visibility, use a see-through or open-toe presser foot.
- If you wish to trim the seam allowance after you have sewn a seam, fold the Vylene back away from the fabric so that you do not accidentally cut it.
- One or two seams at a time can be finger-pressed down but for the sake of accuracy it is best to iron each seam as you go.
- Always over- rather than under-estimate the size of a piece of fabric.

Ironing

Ironing is an important part of the piecing process. Use an iron that has steam capacity but only set it to iron cotton. Iron the stitching in the seam flat before ironing the seam away to one side. This will settle the fibres of the stitching and ensure that the seam is ironed flat. Set the seam with a burst of steam and iron in the direction of the fabric grain.

Quilt top preparation

To mark grid lines (also called hatching, for horizontal and vertical lines or 'cross-hatching', for diagonal lines), measure the sides of the quilt top and find a number that you can easily divide this measurement by. Then mark this measurement at intervals on each side and at the top and the bottom of the quilt or in both directions diagonally and join the marks with straight lines. This type of quilting brings an appliqué or pieced shape into relief.

Stencils

A traditional way to mark the quilt top is by using a stencil. For machine quilting, quilting lines need to be as continuous as possible (for this reason, most machine quilting patterns are also called 'continuous quilting patterns'). Continuous lines make quilting easier as well as stronger.

Enlarge or reduce a pattern chosen from a workbook by using a photocopier, then mark the design onto tulle with a permanent marking pen. Rinse the tulle under water to remove residual ink, then trace the design onto the quilt top with a marking tool.

Another method of tracing a quilting pattern is to glue the correct size pattern to an old X-ray, cut out the pattern and place this template on top of the quilt and trace around it. A light box can also be used to trace a design on a quilt top.

Markers

Quilting pencils are often hard to see under the sewing machine light. Water-soluble pencils, which are available in many colors, are easy to use and see even under the light from the sewing machine. White water-soluble pencils are good for dark fabrics.

Water-soluble pens (especially blue) are also easy to see under machine light and are good for using on light to medium backgrounds. Be aware, however, that heat, such as from an iron, will set water-soluble marked lines.

Care must be taken to wash marks out completely when a quilt is finished.

Victoriana

A foundation block with a diamond motif is bordered by rectangular units of pictorial fabric. Sashing strips with contrasting squares in a small print fabric frame the design.

The floral feature fabric chosen for this quilt is from a range of fabrics with a wedding theme. A reproduction co-ordinating fabric was used as well. These romantic designs lend an old-world appearance to the quilt. With this timeless quality, it is a strong contender for becoming a family heirloom.

Finished size For a throw rug (171 x 206 cm; 67 x 81 in)

Materials
Foundation blocks
◆ Enough fabric for twenty-four center diamonds measuring 5 x 3½ in (127 x 90 mm) (Fabric A). (It is a good idea to make a plastic template of the center diamond and take it with you when you go to purchase the fabric.) The amount of fabric you purchase will depend on the print you select for the center of this block. The most suitable fabrics are small or medium prints

The next three types of fabric should co-ordinate with Fabric A:
◆ 15¾ in (40 cm) of fabric to surround Fabric A (Fabric B)
◆ 31½ in (80 cm) of fabric to surround Fabric B (Fabric C)
◆ 59 in (1.5 meters) of fabric to surround Fabric C (Fabric D)

Feature block
◆ Enough fabric for twenty-five blocks measuring 7½ x 5½ in (190 x 140 mm). Pictorial fabrics with medium or large prints are suitable. The fabric should complement the center diamond fabric. The amount of fabric will depend upon the type of print. If you want to use an 'all over' pattern, you will need to purchase 1 yard (1 meter) of fabric

Borders and sashing
◆ 33½ in (85 cm) of fabric for the first border. Choose a tone-on-one contrasting fabric that will enhance and frame the blocks
◆ 4 in (10 cm) of fabric for sashing squares. If you decide to put the sashing squares in the quilt you will need a contrast small print fabric.
◆ 10 in (25 cm) of fabric for the second border (you could use Fabric C fabric)
◆ 39 in (1 m) of fabric for the third border (you could use Fabric D fabric)
◆ Twenty-five appliqué broderie perse motifs (you should use the same fabric that you use for the feature blocks)
◆ 79 in (2 m) of fabric for the fourth border. This is a feature border and really is the focus of the entire quilt. It probably will be the first fabric you choose. You should use it to select the co-ordinating fabrics
◆ 27½ in (70 cm) of binding fabric

LEFT Elegant but understated, the quilt looks wonderful in a traditional interior. The delicate floral feature fabric provides charm and adds interest.

Other

◆ 4½ yd (4 m) of backing fabric
◆ 2½ x 2¼ yd (2.2 x 2 m) of batting
◆ 1½ yd (1.5 m) of non-fusible interfacing of medium weight
◆ HB-type lead pencil
◆ Thin, plastic 12 in (30 cm) long ruler
◆ Blu-Tack

◆ Template plastic
◆ Threads to match
◆ Ruler, rotary cutter and mat
◆ Flower pins
◆ Invisible monofilament thread
◆ 1 meter of double-sided fusible webbing for appliqué
◆ 1 meter of appliqué tearaway

Foundation block template

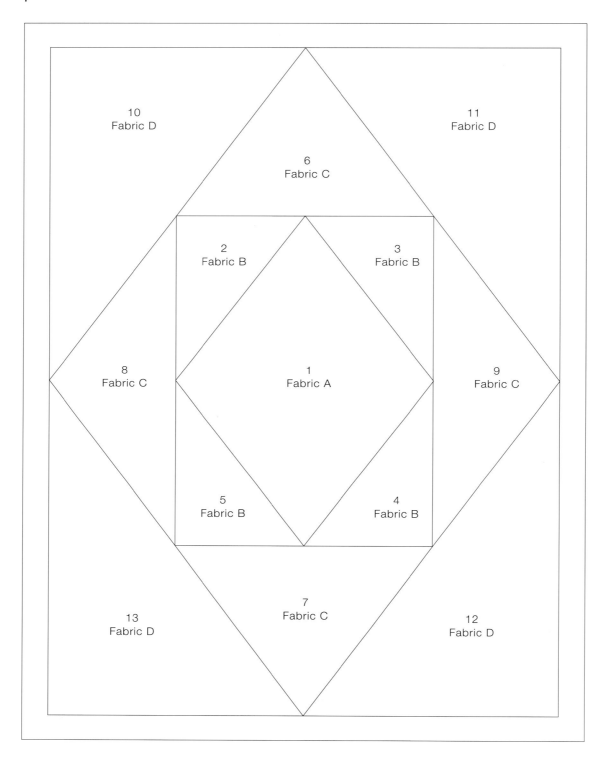

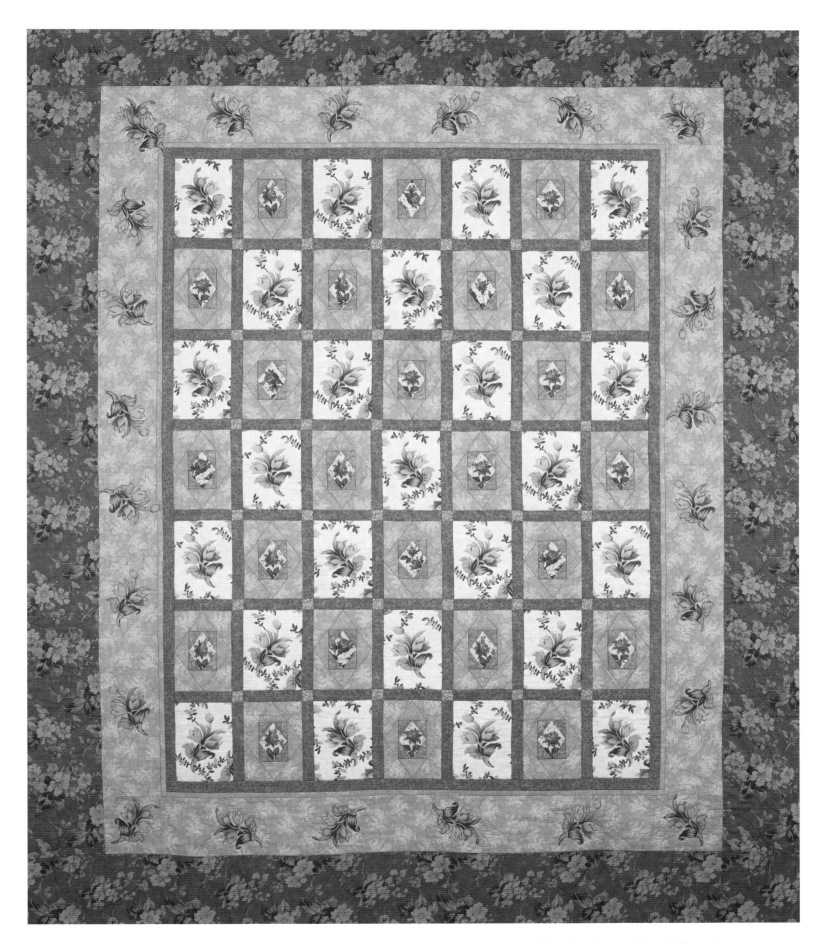

Splashes of red and blue enliven the quilt's warm, muted color scheme. The simple geometric design of rectangles and diamonds showcases the charming feature fabric.

METHOD

1 Using the template on page 64, trace twenty-four foundation blocks onto medium-weight interfacing using a pencil and ruler. Secure the pattern and interfacing while tracing with a small amount of Blu-Tack. You could also photocopy the pattern twenty-four times instead and sew it to the paper. However, if you choose this method, it's best to use a laser photocopier because other photocopiers tend to distort images. You will need to remove the paper from the block when the top is complete.

2 Trace the center diamond onto template plastic, add a ¼ in (6 mm) seam and trim off the four corner points to ¼ in (6 mm).

3 Cut twenty-four center diamonds by aligning the plastic template over the design on Fabric A.

4 Cut four 3 in (76 mm) strips across the width of Fabric B. Cut these strips into forty-eight 3 in (76 mm) squares. Then cut each square diagonally to make ninety-six triangles.

5 Cut pieces from Fabric C. For the top and bottom triangular pieces, cut four 3 in (76 mm) strips across the width of the fabric. Cut these into forty-eight 3½ in (90 mm) rectangles. For the triangles at the sides, cut six 2½ in (63 mm) strips across the width of the fabric. Cut these into forty-eight 4½ in (115 mm) rectangles.

6 Cut sixteen 3½ in (90 mm) strips across the width of Fabric D. Cut these into ninety-six 6 in (152 mm) rectangles.

7 On Panel 1, pin Fabric A right side up on the wrong side of the foundation block. (Note: All other pieces are to be pinned right side down. Once sewn, they will be folded over along the seam line and pressed.)

8 Fold along the line between Panels 1 and 2, pin Fabric B right sides together over the crease mark and sew on the line, making sure there is at least ¼ in (6 mm) of fabric for the seam allowance. (You can check this by holding the work up to the light.) Turn the work over. Start and finish sewing ¼ in (6 mm) beyond the drawn line. Trim both fabrics to a neat ¼ in (6 mm) seam and press open gently with a warm iron. (Make sure that the iron is not too hot or it will shrink the interfacing.)

9 Sew each of the other panels in numerical order. When the block is finished, sew around the block inside the ¼ in (6 mm) seam allowance. Then, with the right side facing, carefully trim the block to 5½ x 7½ in (140 x 190 mm), allowing a ¼ in (6 mm) seam around the block. Make sure that you have a ¼ in (6 mm) seam allowance on every point.

10 Cut twenty-five 7½ x 5½ in (190 x 140 mm) feature blocks from the feature border fabric. You could make a plastic template so you can center the pattern on the fabric.

Sewing the sashing pieces to the blocks

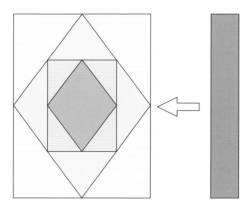

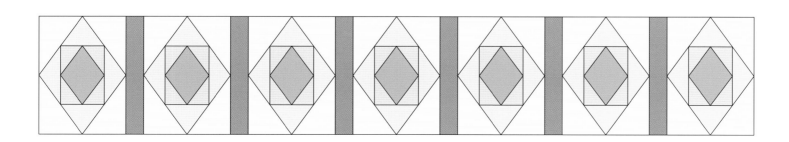

11 For the sashing, cut fifteen 1½ in (38 mm) strips, across the width of the fabric. Crosscut these to make forty-two 7½ in (190 mm) rectangles and forty-two 5½ in (140 mm) rectangles. Cut a 1½ in (38 mm) strip from sashing square fabric, across the width of the fabric. Crosscut it into thirty-six 1½ in (38 mm) squares. Referring to the diagram, sew a 7½ in (190 mm) sashing rectangle to a feature or foundation block. (There are seven blocks and six sashing rectangles.) Press the seams towards the sashing. Repeat this process seven times.

12 Sew seven 5½ in (140 mm) strips to six 1½ in (38 mm) squares. Press seams towards the sashing. Repeat this process six times.

Sewing the 5½ and 1½ in sashing pieces

13 Sew the joined blocks following the quilt design. Press all seams towards the sashing.

14 Cut five 1½ in (38 mm) strips from the sashing fabric for the first border. Cut five 1 in (25 mm) strips from the second border fabric. Cut six 5½ in (140 mm) strips from the third border fabric. Cut four 7½ in (190 mm) strips the length of the fabric to the measurements of the quilt for the fourth border. Cut eight 3 in (76 mm) strips from the binding fabric.

15 Measure through the center of the quilt when adding all the following borders. This will keep the quilt straight and square. For the first border, join two strips and cut to the length of the quilt. Sew to one side of the quilt. Press seams towards the border. Repeat for the other side. Join two strips and, measuring horizontally, through the center of the quilt, cut to this measurement. Sew to the top. Repeat for the bottom of the quilt. Press seams towards the border. Square each corner.

16 For the second border, measure vertically through the center of the quilt. Join two strips and cut to the measurement. Sew to one side of the quilt. Repeat for the other side. Press seams towards the first border. Join two

strips and cut to the width of the quilt. Sew to the top of the quilt. Repeat for the bottom of the quilt. Press seams towards the first border. Square each corner.

17 For the third border, measure vertically, through the center of the quilt. Join two strips and cut to this measurement then sew to one side of the quilt. Repeat for the other side. Press seams towards the third border. Join two strips twice and cut each joined piece to the width of the quilt. Sew one piece to the top and one piece to the bottom of the quilt. Press seams towards the third border. Square each corner.

18 For the fourth border, measure vertically, through the center of the quilt, adding 2 in (50 mm), and cut the lengthwise strip to this measurement for both sides. Place a pin 1 in (25 mm) from each end. (Sometimes when cutting the fabric lengthwise, the fabric will not give and you need a little extra to fit the side of the quilt. If this happens, make sure both sides are the same.) Measure through the center of the quilt and add the top and bottom borders in the same manner. Square the corners.

19 To attach the appliqué pieces, iron Vliesofix to the back of the motifs and cut out the required number of designs to place around the quilt in the third border. Iron the pieces to the border. Iron appliqué tearaway to the back of the border to stabilize it while appliquéing. Using invisible monofilament thread appliqué the motifs using a small zigzag stitch.

TO FINISH

20 Layer the quilt and pin or tack ready for quilting. Quilt in-the-ditch around the foundation block, feature block and borders. Quilt the foundation block and feature block design. Trace a stencil design on the fourth border and quilt. Join the eight binding strips using 45 degree seams, fold in half and press lengthwise. Trim the quilt along the edges, making sure the width of the last border is the same all around the quilt. Starting halfway along the bottom border, using the walking foot, sew the binding to the quilt, remembering to mitre the corners. Fold the binding to the back of the quilt and slip stitch by hand with a matching thread. Label the quilt.

Pieced and Appliquéd Medallion

Pastel colors and curved, free-flowing shapes create a feeling of brightness and ease. Patchwork border blocks frame the appliqué feature pattern.

This small quilt is created using both the patchwork and the mock appliqué technique. The design, which features medallion motifs and Ohio Star blocks, is embellished with an array of quilting patterns.

Finished size For the lap or a wall (153 x 153 cm; 60 x 60 in)

Materials

◆ 3 yd (2.75 m) of background material
◆ ½ yd (40 cm) of five different medium blue prints
◆ ½ yd (40 cm) of five different medium light blue prints
◆ Fat ⅛ of three different cream with blue floral prints (light prints)
◆ Fat ⅛ of five different yellow prints (light prints)
◆ ⅝ yd (50 cm) of green fabric (light)
◆ ¼ yd (20 cm) of blue fabric for the first border
◆ ¼ yd (20 cm) of blue fabric for the third border
◆ ⅓ yd (30 cm) of blue fabric for the fifth border
◆ ⅝ yd (50 cm) of blue fabric for the seventh border
◆ 3⅛ yd (2.8 m) of backing fabric
◆ 1¾ yd of continuous 90 in wide wadding (1.6 m of continuous 2.2 m wide wadding)

◆ ⅝ yd (50 cm) of fabric for binding
◆ 3¼ yd (3 m) of freezer paper
◆ Water-soluble adhesive stick
◆ Lead pencil, a pair of scissors for paper and a pair of scissors for fabric (or appliqué)
◆ Sewing machine
◆ Clear 004 monofilament thread for the top of the sewing machine
◆ Quilting thread (to match the background fabric) for the bobbin
◆ ⅝ yd (50 cm) of white tulle

CUTTING THE FABRIC

1 From each of four medium blue prints, cut one 3¼ in (83 mm) strip. Recut into thirteen 3¼ in (83 mm) squares (for the border and the Ohio Stars). (Note: You will probably only obtain twelve 3¼ in/83 mm squares per width of fabric and will need to cut an extra 3¼ in/83 mm square. Allowance has been made for this.) Cut a 2½ in (63 mm) strip. Recut into three 2½ in (63 mm) squares for the center stars.

2 From the remaining medium blue print, cut one 3¼ in (83 mm) strip. Recut into eleven 3¼ in (83 mm) squares for the border and the Ohio Stars. Cut a 2½ in (63 mm) strip. Recut into two 2½ in (63 mm) squares for the center stars.

3 Choose the three darkest of the medium light blue prints. From each of the three fabrics, cut one 3¼ in (83 mm) strip. Recut into eleven 3¼ in (83 mm) squares for the border and the Ohio Stars. Cut one 2½ in (63 mm) strip. Recut into two 2½ in (63 mm) squares for the center Ohio Stars. (Note: In four of the medium blue fabrics, you will have three Ohio Star blocks and in the remaining four fabrics (a medium blue and three medium light blues), you will have only two Ohio Star blocks.)

4 For the background, cut eight 3¼ in (83 mm) lengths. Recut into ninety-two 3¼ in (83 mm) squares for the quarter-square triangle blocks. Cut five 2½ in (63 mm) lengths. Recut into eighty 2½ in (63 mm) squares for the corners in the Ohio Star blocks. Cut one 24½ in (622 mm) square for the center. This will be cut down later to

RIGHT The quilt's medallion motifs and Ohio Star blocks give it a colonial flavor, while its pretty pastel colors imbue it with cottage charm.

become a 22½ in (572 mm) square. Cut six 6½ in (165 mm) strips. Join together on the bias to make one continuous length. Recut the continuous length into two 6½ x 38½ in (165 x 980 mm) lengths and two 6½ x 50½ in (165 x 129 mm) lengths for the fourth border.

5 For the first border, cut four 1½ in (38 mm) lengths. Recut two 1½ in (38 mm) lengths into twenty-two ½ in (13 mm) lengths. Recut the other two 1½ in (38 mm) lengths into twenty-four ½ in (13 mm) lengths.

6 For the third border, cut four 1½ in (38 mm) strips. Recut two 1½ in (38 m) lengths into thirty-six ½ in (13 mm) lengths. Recut the other two 1½ in (38 mm) lengths into thirty-eight ½ in (13 mm) lengths.

7 For the fifth border, cut six 1½ in (38 mm) lengths. Join together on the bias to make one continuous length. Cut the continuous length into two 1½ x 50½ in (38 mm x 128 cm) and two 1½ x 52½ in (38 mm x 133 cm) lengths.

8 For the seventh border, cut six 2½ in (63 mm) lengths. Join together on the bias to make one continuous length. Cut the continuous length into two 2½ x 56½ in (63 mm x 144 cm) lengths and two 2½ x 60½ in (63 mm x 154 cm) lengths.

9 For the binding, cut seven 2¼ in (57 mm) lengths. Join together on the bias to make one continuous length.

10 From the green fabric, cut one 10 in (254 mm) square for the center bias circle vine. Cut one 19 in (483 mm) square for the border bias vine strip. Following the Cutting the Green Fabric diagram and the instructions below, prepare both squares to make the vine for the center and the border. Fold the square in half diagonally in each direction and press a crease in each of the folds. Cut along one diagonal crease (Step 1 of the diagram). Sew two halves together with a ¼ in (6 mm) seam (Step 2 of the diagram). Press the seam open. With the ruler, mark lines in 1½ in (38 mm) widths across the binding strip. With right sides together and making a ¼ in (6 mm) seam, sew the binding strip into a tube so that X and Y match (see Step 3 of the diagram) and the lines are in alignment. Iron the seam open. Cut along the line, which will appear to be continuous. Iron the prepared length in half, wrong sides together, down the entire length of the bias strip. Sew a ¼ in (6 mm) seam down the raw edge and, using a ½ in (13 mm) bias bar, iron the tubes so that the seam is hidden underneath.

Cutting the green fabric

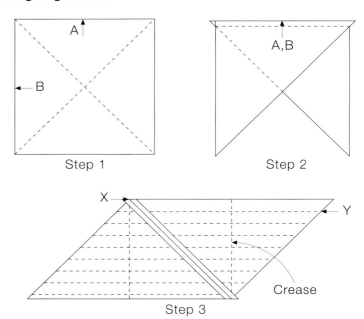

Step 1

Step 2

Step 3

Crease

CUTTING THE APPLIQUE

11 From freezer paper, cut thirteen Large Flower templates (see page 73). Cut seventy-eight Large Flower Petal (six for each large flower) templates. Cut thirteen Large Flower Center templates. Cut twenty-nine Small Flower templates. Cut twenty-nine Small Inner Flower templates. Cut twenty-nine Small Flower Center templates.

12 Using the freezer paper templates, match:
■ Medium blue prints: Three fabrics to three Large Flower freezer paper templates and two fabrics to two Large Flower freezer paper templates. Four fabrics to six Small Flower Center freezer paper templates and one fabric to five Small Flower Center freezer paper templates.
■ Medium light blue prints: Four fabrics to six Small Flower freezer paper templates, and one fabric to five Small Flower freezer paper templates.
■ Cream with blue floral prints: Two fabrics to twenty-four Large Flower Petal (eight flowers in total) freezer paper templates, one fabric to thirty Large Flower Petal (five flowers) freezer paper templates. (Note: You can also use one or two of the lightest medium light blues.)
■ Yellows: Four fabrics to six Small Inner Flower freezer paper templates, one fabric to five Small Inner Flower freezer paper templates, three fabrics to three Large Flower Center freezer paper templates and two fabrics to two Large Flower Center templates.

APPLIQUEING

You may appliqué using any method. The instructions here are for mock appliqué.

Its appearance may suggest otherwise, but the quilt-top design is quite involved and requires some time and patience to create. Seven borders and numerous motifs add to its complexity.

13 Trace the template design onto the paper side of the freezer paper. Carefully cut out the shape with scissors for paper, making sure that the cuts are very smooth because uneven edges will appear on the finished appliqué. Make sure that you have all the pieces at hand to make a flower (that is, one Large Flower template, six Large Flower Petal templates and one Large Flower Center template, or one

Small Flower template, one Small Inner Flower template and one Small Flower Center template.

14 Iron the shiny side of each freezer paper template to the wrong side of the chosen fabric, making sure that there is a good ½ in (13 mm) between one template shape and the next.

15 Using fabric scissors (or appliqué scissors), cut the fabric around each freezer paper template, adding a scant ¼ in (6 mm) seam allowance. Snip in the centers of the petal edges to within a few threads of the freezer paper template.

16 Using a water-soluble adhesive stick, glue the fabric seam allowance around a freezer paper template. Using the top, and not the side, of the thumb, press the seam allowance down. Repeat for each piece of the flower.

17 Using the pattern as a guide, place and layer the prepared appliqué pieces to form a completed flower.

18 Using the blind hem stitch function on the machine, and (if possible) with the straight part of the stitch on the right, set the width and length to approximately 1.

19 Thread the machine with monofilament thread, release the tension and place a size 60 or 70 needle in the machine. Use an open-toe embroidery foot or use a clear plastic foot so that you can watch the needle.

20 Place quilting thread to match the background in the bobbin. (Note: You may need to tighten the tension on the bobbin if releasing the top tension is not enough to anchor the stitch evenly.)

21 Position the prepared flower under the foot so that the right-hand straight stitch component of the blind hem stitch stitches into the background (or the back of the template piece) and the left-hand 'swing' component of the blind hem stitch catches only three to four threads of the prepared templates. Using continuous stitching, appliqué all the pieces onto the flower. Repeat until there are thirteen large flowers and twenty-nine small flowers. (This will require practice, as each sewing machine is different. When you are satisfied with the stitch, write down the specifications of the stitch and the tension so that when you do the stitch again you will be able to set up the machine quickly.)

22 After the appliqué has been sewn onto the quilt, from the back of the quilt, using the stitching as a guide, cut a good ¼ in (6 mm) away from the stitching, spray the area with water, wait a minute or two, then remove the freezer paper from the appliqué by pulling up the edge of the freezer paper with an unpicker.

23 Iron the square from the back, then turn the temperature of the iron down and iron from the front.

24 To mark the appliqué pattern onto the center block and border, photocopy the pattern for the center block (see sheet C of the fold-out sheets in the center of this book). With a permanent laundry marker, trace the photocopied pattern onto the tulle. Wash the marked tulle under cold water to remove any residue from the permanent marker. Place the prepared tulle over the center block and, using a water-soluble pen, mark the pattern guide onto the block. These markings can be used to place the bias vine and the flowers.

25 Repeat the procedure described for the appliquéd fourth border.

26 To form the center block, using the mock appliqué technique, iron the center block vertically, horizontally and vertically again. These creases will be used to help you match the pattern to the block. Place the prepared tulle into position, matching up the pattern markings, and mark the center block with the vine and flower positions using water-soluble ink. Prepare a bias strip from the 10 in (254 mm) square and, using the circle on the center square as a guide, pin it in place and then appliqué it down using the mock appliqué technique. Place the prepared flowers into position on the background square and appliqué down. Do not cut the backgrounds away at this stage. Leave that until the entire quilt top is finished.

27 To appliqué the fourth border using the mock appliqué technique, mark a center point along each side of it (this will be approximately 25 in/635 mm in from each edge). Using the prepared tulle, mark the border with the vine and flower positions using a water-soluble pen. (You may have to 'fudge' the pattern a little to get it to fit the quilt top. Do this by scrunching the tulle to fit into the measured area. You will find that you may have to scrunch about ¼ in (6 mm), which is quite easy to do over a 25 in/ 635 mm length.) Prepare a bias strip (from the 19 in/ 483 mm square) and cut into eight equal lengths. Use two lengths per side. Using the pattern as a guide, pin the vine in place, and then appliqué down using the mock appliqué technique and the pattern as a guide. Place the prepared flowers into position on the background border and appliqué down. Once again, do not cut the backgrounds away.

PIECING

28 You will need 184, 2 in (50 mm) (finished) quarter-square triangle blocks for the whole quilt, including for the Ohio Stars and the border. For the background of these triangle blocks, you need ninety-two, 3¼ in (83 mm)

LARGE FLOWER TEMPLATES

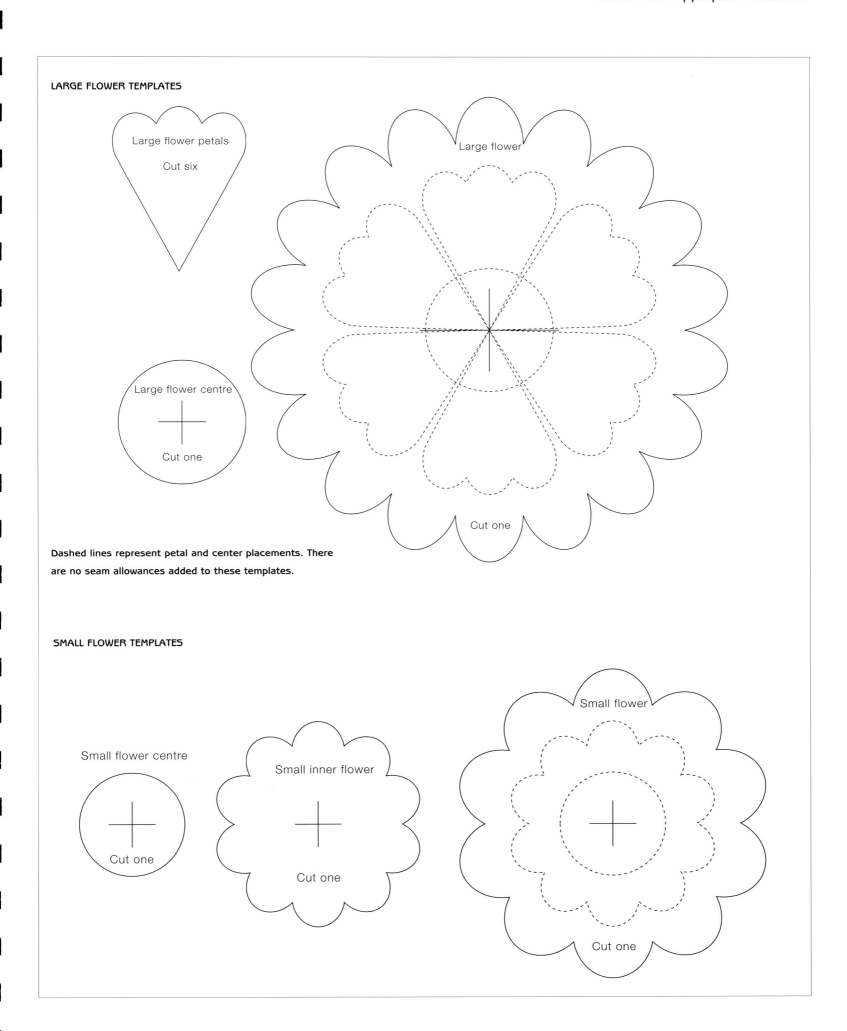

Large flower petals

Cut six

Large flower centre

Cut one

Large flower

Cut one

Dashed lines represent petal and center placements. There are no seam allowances added to these templates.

SMALL FLOWER TEMPLATES

Small flower centre

Cut one

Small inner flower

Cut one

Small flower

Cut one

squares. For the blue sections, you need ninety-two, 3¼ in (83 mm) squares in eight different blue fabrics. Start by taking two 3¼ in (83 mm) squares, one background and one blue square. Draw a diagonal line from corner to corner on the background square. Put both squares together, with right sides touching. Stitch ¼ in (6 mm) away on both sides of the drawn line. Cut on the line and iron towards the blue. You will form two half-square triangle blocks. (Note: These blocks will measure ⅞ in/ 22 mm more than the finished size.) Draw a diagonal line from corner to corner across the seam on one of the half-square triangle blocks. Put both half-square triangle blocks together, making sure that you match opposite colors to each other and seam to seam (make sure you can feel them lock together). Once again, stitch ¼ in (6 mm) away on both sides of the line. Cut on the line and iron in one direction. Repeat (always matching a background square to a blue square) until you have 184, 2 in (50 mm) finished blocks.

MAKING THE QUARTER-SQUARE TRIANGLE BLOCKS

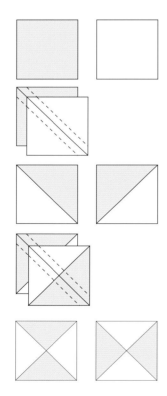

29 The quilt requires twenty blocks of Ohio Stars. Each star is made of four 2½ in (63 mm) background squares, one 2½ in (63 mm) star center and four matching quarter-square triangle blocks which form the points of the star. Referring to the Making an Ohio Star diagram below, sew a 2½ in (63 mm) background square to both sides of a quarter-square triangle block. Iron in the direction of

MAKING AN OHIO STAR

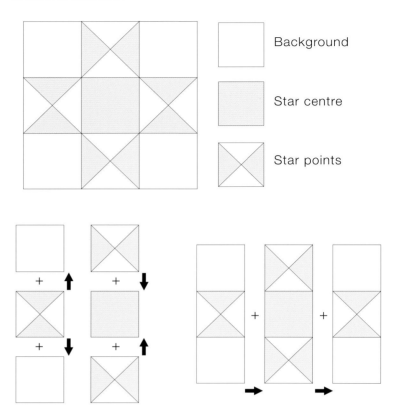

arrows. Make another of these units. Sew a quarter-square triangle block to both sides of a 2½ in (63 mm) center square, making sure that the feature (or background) is next to the center square. Iron in the direction of the arrows. Sew a quarter-square triangle block/background square unit to a quarter-square triangle block/center square unit to the other quarter-square triangle block/background square unit. Iron in the direction of arrows. Repeat the entire procedure to make twenty Ohio Star blocks. Remember to construct three identical Ohio Stars in four groups of color and two identical Ohio Stars in four alternative groups of color.

30 Referring to the diagram below, make the pieced sixth border. Use the thirteen quarter-square triangle blocks remaining in eight groups of color. Arrange the eight groups of color in an order that you like. Join a quarter-square triangle block in each color group together, making sure that you have the blue shades meeting. Iron towards the darkest blue. Make thirteen of these. Join the thirteen sections together, making sure they are in the same order. You should now have one continuous strip. Count twenty-six quarter-square triangle blocks along, and open the seam between it and the twenty-seventh quarter-square triangle block. Mark this as the 'top'. Mark the first quarter-square triangle block as 'left' and the sixth quarter-square triangle block as 'right'. Repeat this process by counting another twenty-six quarter-square triangle blocks along, and open the seam between this and the twenty-seventh quarter-square triangle block. Mark this 'right side', again marking the left and the right. Repeat this procedure two more times until you have a bottom and a left side.

31 To form the corner squares, cut four 2⅞ in (73 mm) squares in background fabric and cut one 2⅞ in (73 mm) square in the first, third, fifth and seventh fabric used in the first step of point 30 above. Make half-square triangle blocks, matching a background square to each blue fabric. You should end up with two half-square triangle blocks in each color (eight in total), but will use only one of each (four in total). Match the fifth color half-square triangle block to the left side of the top section and the seventh color half-square triangle block to the right side of the top section.

32 Match the first color half-square triangle block to the left side of the bottom section and the third color half-square triangle block to the right side of the bottom section. (Note: The pieced section goes around the quilt in order, so that the order of the blocks is unbroken. This means that when the bottom piece is sewn onto the quilt top, it will appear to be upside down on the quilt. The piece is not to be seen as on the quilt. If this were so, the first color half-square triangle block would be on the right-hand side of the quilt and the third color half-square triangle block would be on the left-hand side of the quilt.)

ASSEMBLING THE QUILT TOP

33 After appliquéing the center block, cut the block down to a 22½ in (57 cm) square. Add all of the borders as follows:

■ First border: Sew the two 1½ in (38 mm) x width of

PIECED SIXTH BORDER

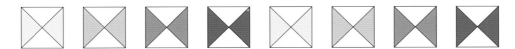

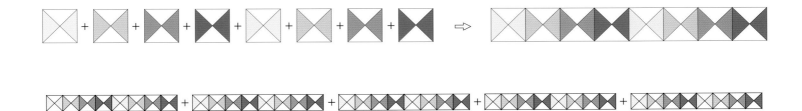

CORNER SQUARES

75

fabric lengths to form 22½ in (57 cm) lengths and sew to the sides of the appliqué block. Sew the two 1½ in (38 mm) x width of fabric lengths to form 24½ in (62 cm) lengths and sew to the top and bottom of the appliqué block.

■ Second border: Form two strips of four Ohio Star blocks. Sew the strips to the sides of the quilt top. Make two strips of six Ohio Star blocks. Sew one strip to the top and the other to the bottom of the quilt top. Note: The seam allowances go in one direction. To lock the second block into the first block's seams, turn the second block upside down. Follow this procedure to fit all of the blocks together.

■ Third border: Sew two 1½ in (38 mm) x width of fabric lengths to form 36½ in (93 cm) lengths and sew each length to one side of the quilt top. Sew the two 1½ in (38 mm) x width of fabric strips to form 38½ in (98 cm) lengths and sew a strip to the top and another to the bottom of the quilt top.

■ Fourth border: Sew the two 6½ x 38½ in (165 mm x 98 cm) lengths to the sides of the quilt top. Sew a 6½ x 50½ in (165 mm x 128 cm) length to the top of the quilt top and the other 6½ x 50½ in (165 mm x 128 cm) length to the bottom of the quilt top.

■ Fifth border: Sew each of the two 1½ x 50½ in (38 mm x 128 cm) lengths to a side of the quilt top. Sew a 1½ x 52½ in (38 mm x 133 cm) length to the top of the quilt top and the other 1½ x 52½ in (38 mm x 133 cm) length to the bottom of the quilt top.

■ Sixth border: Gather the pieced, sixth border sections. Sew the left-hand side section to the left-hand side of the quilt top ('left' should be to your left and 'right' to your right). Sew the right-hand side section to the right-hand side of the quilt top ('left' is to your left and 'right' to your right). Sew the top section to the top of the quilt top (the left-hand side section and the fifth color half-square triangle block should be to your left and the right-hand side section and the seventh color half-square triangle block should be to your right as you attach it to the quilt top). Sew the bottom section to the bottom of the quilt top (the left-hand side section and the first color half-square triangle block should be to your left and the right-hand side section and the third color half-square triangle block should be to your right as you attach it to the quilt top).

■ Seventh border: Sew the two 2½ x 56½ in (63 mm x 144 cm) lengths to the sides of the quilt top. Sew a 2½ x 60½ in (63 mm x 154 cm) length to the top and the other to the bottom of the quilt top.

34 Referring to the Design photograph (see page 71), sew the green bias strips onto the fourth border. Place the prepared large and small flowers in position and appliqué down.

35 Cut away the seam allowance at the back of the quilt top and remove the paper from the center block and the border.

MARKING THE QUILT TOP

36 Test the marking pen or pencil on a scrap of background fabric, then mark the entire quilt top. Using the diagonal seam lines of the second and the sixth border quarter-square triangle blocks as a guide, draw diagonal grid lines in the outside edge of the center block and the background of the appliquéd fourth border. Referring to the Half-size Center Block Layout and Placement Guide on sheet C of the fold-out sheets in the center of this book, mark the center of the appliqué circle.

37 From the backing 3⅛ yd (286 cm) length, cut a 67 in (170 cm) length of fabric (see step 1 of the diagram on page 75). Cut two 21½ in (55 cm) lengths (see step 2 of the diagram). Join these lengths together end to end (see step 3 of the diagram) and sew the new length to one side of the 67 in (170 cm) length. Cut off the excess fabric and iron all the seams open (see step 4 of the diagram).

38 Cut the batting down to a 66 x 66 in (168 x 168 cm) or join pieces of batting together to make to a piece this size.

BACKING

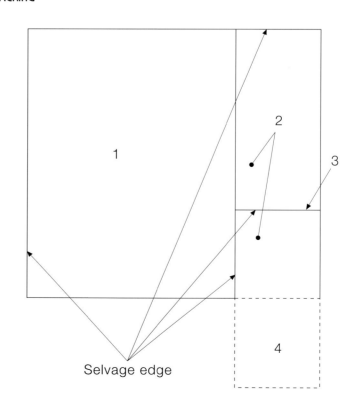

Selvage edge

39 Place the layers of the quilt together. Quilt in-the-ditch around all the borders, the stars in the second border and the quarter-square triangle and half-square triangle blocks in the fourth border. Then quilt along the grid lines in the center block and in the fourth border.

40 Quilt in-the-ditch around the vines and each flower shape. You could also quilt around the centers of the flowers.

41 To bind the quilt, iron the 2¼ in (57 mm) continuous lengths in half, wrong sides together, down their entire lengths. With the raw edges of the binding matching the raw edge of the quilt, sew the binding to the quilt. Hand or machine stitch in place.

42 Prepare a label for the back of the quilt. Make a sleeve for hanging the quilt using the piece of backing that remains.

Pieced and Appliquéd Medallion makes a superb wallhanging in a contemporary country-style room.

Road to California

While this quilt is not created from scraps, the Road to California design can be constructed from odd pieces of fabric.

The Road to California design dates back to 1849 and heralds the arrival of the first railroads and the gold rush in America. It is an easy quilt to piece, and the red and cream color combination is very effective. In this version, the traditional color pattern has been reversed.

Finished size For a double bed (190 cm x 237; 75 x 93 in)

Materials

◆ White fabric: 2¾ yd (2.5 m) for blocks; 2½ yd (2.35 m) for lattice strips; ¾ yd (70 cm) for binding; 7½ yd (7 m) homespun or quilters muslin for backing
◆ 2 yd (1.8 m) of red spotted fabric
◆ 1 yd (90 cm) of red plaid fabric
◆ 2 yd (1.8 m) of red floral fabric
◆ Queen size (85 x 103 in) wadding
◆ Rotary cutter
◆ Rotary board and ruler

LEFT Smart cream and red fabrics in plaids and spots make this quilt the focus of a room. The Road to California quilt looks best in an interior that is simply furnished.

CUTTING THE FABRIC

Note: Cut all fabric selvage to selvage. The seam allowance used throughout is ¼ in (6 mm). Press all seams towards the dark side.

1 From the white fabric, cut thirty-three 1½ in (38 mm) strips and thirteen 2½ in (63 mm) strips. Then cut five 15½ in (394 mm) strips and crosscut them into 3½ x 15½ in (90 x 394 mm) strips, to make forty-nine lattice strips.

2 From the red spotted fabric, cut twenty-six 1½ in (38 mm) strips. Cut five 3½ in (90 mm) strips and crosscut into 2½ in (63 mm) strips to make eighty strips.

3 From the red plaid fabric cut three 1½ (38 mm) strips. Cut ten 2½ in (63 mm) strips.

4 From the red floral fabric, cut ten, 1½ in (38 mm) strips. Cut five 3½ in (90 mm) strips and crosscut into 2½ in (63 mm) strips to make eighty strips.

FORMING THE BLOCKS

5 To form nine-patch units from the red spotted and the white fabric, lay out six white, six red spotted and another six white strips. Sew together nine of these units. Press seams towards the dark side then crosscut into 1½ in (38 mm) strips to make 160 strips.

LAYING OUT THE WHITE AND RED SPOTTED STRIPS

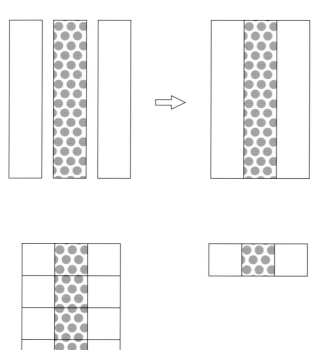

6 Lay out three red spotted, three white and another three red spotted strips. Sew the red, white and red strips together four and a half times. Press seams towards the dark side, then crosscut into 1½ in (38 mm) strips to make eighty strips.

LAYING OUT THE RED SPOTTED AND WHITE STRIPS

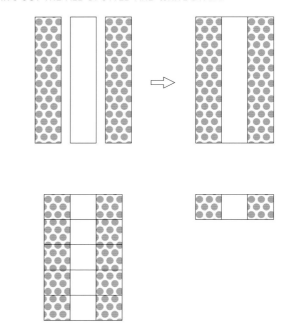

7 Sew the rectangles together to form the nine-patch blocks.

SEWING THE RECTANGLES TOGETHER

8 To form nine-patch units for the corners of the blocks, lay out a 2½ in (63 mm) white, a 2½ in (63 mm) red floral and a 2½ in (63 mm) white strip. Then lay out a 1¼ in (32 mm) red floral, a 1¼ in (32 mm) white and a 1¼ in (32 mm) red floral strip. Sew together in the same way as for steps 6 and 7. This will make thirty nine-patch units for the corners of the blocks.

CREATING THE FOUR-PATCH UNITS

9 From the red spotted and white fabric, sew six red and six white strips together. Press seams towards the dark side of the fabric, then crosscut into 1½ in (38 mm) strips. Referring to the Creating the Four-patch Units diagram below, rotate one of the two strips in each unit 180 degrees and sew the strips together to form 80 units.

Constructed largely of nine-patch blocks, this version of the Road to California quilt is quite easy to create.

CREATING THE FOUR-PATCH UNITS

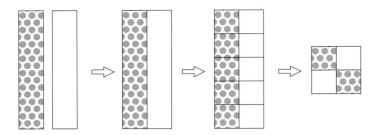

LAYING OUT THE UNITS

10 Lay out six 2½ in (63 mm) red plaid, six 1½ in (38 mm) white and six 2½ in (63 mm) red plaid strips. Press seams and sew together.

LAYING OUT THE RED PLAID AND WHITE STRIPS

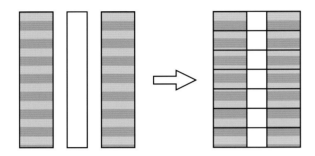

11 Lay out six 2½ in (63 mm) white, six 1½ in (38 mm) red plaid and six 2½ in (63 mm) white strips. Press seams and sew together.

LAYING OUT THE WHITE AND RED PLAID STRIPS

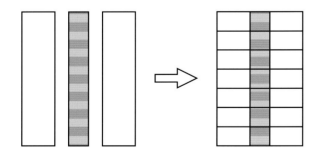

12 Crosscut into 1½ in (38 mm) strips and sew two rectangles together. This will make eighty units.

SEWING TWO RECTANGLES TOGETHER

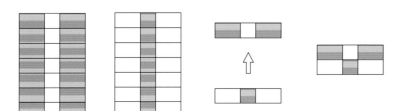

MAKING THE CENTER NINE-PATCH

13 Lay out two-and-a-half strips each of 2½ in (63 mm) white, 1½ in (38 mm) red floral and 2½ in (63 mm) white fabric. Sew together and press seams towards the dark side of the fabric. Crosscut into 2½ in (63 mm) strips. This will make forty units. Lay out one-and-a-quarter strips each of 2½ in (63 mm) red floral, 1½ in (38 mm) white and 2½ in (63 mm) red floral fabric and sew together. Press seams and crosscut into 1½ in (38 mm) strips. Lay out the strips and sew together to make twenty nine-patch units.

MAKING TWENTY NINE-PATCH UNITS

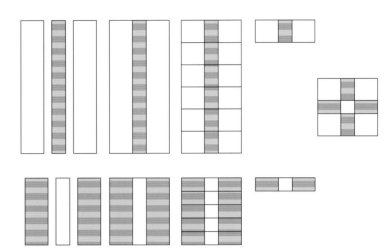

ASSEMBLING THE BLOCKS

14 Place the units and rectangles in position. Sew together, pressing as you sew.

ASSEMBLING THE MAIN BLOCK

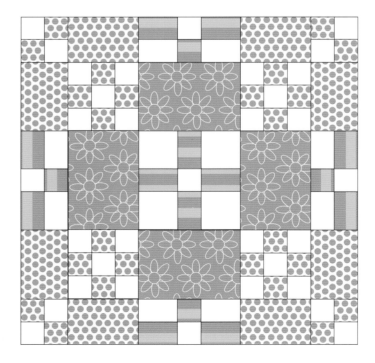

COMPLETING THE QUILT TOP

15 Beginning and ending with a red floral nine-patch, sew lattice strips and nine patches in six rows of four across. Then sew a lattice strip to the left-hand side of the block and another on the right-hand side of the end block. Sew the rows together to form four blocks across and five blocks down.

16 Lay the backing fabric down wrong side up, place the wadding on top and, leaving 2 in (50 mm) around the edge, place the quilt top on these. Clamp the assembled pieces to a table to make quilting smoother and easier. If you are quilting by machine, pin the pieces together with safety pins. Baste the pieces, if quilting by hand.

BINDING THE QUILT

17 Cut the binding fabric into 2¾ in (70 mm) strips. Sew enough strips together to take up the length of the sides, then enough to fit across the top and the bottom of the quilt.

18 For each edge of the quilt, press the strip's seams to the wrong side, place the raw edge of the quilt top and a raw edge of the strip together and sew ¼ in (6 mm) from the edge.

19 Cut the wadding and the backing fabric back to ½ in (13 mm) from the stitching line and then fold the binding over to the back of the quilt. Slip stitch the binding in place.

SEWING THE LATTICE STRIPS

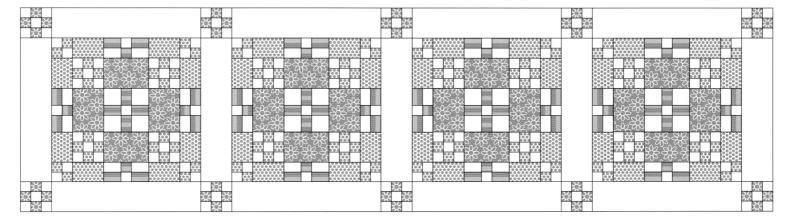

MAKING SLEEVES

A quilt designed to be displayed on a wall should have a sleeve on the back, to hold a rod. A sleeve is also useful on a bed quilt, in case it is decided that the quilt be used for decoration.

   To make a sleeve, follow the steps below.
■ Select a piece of fabric 6 to 8 in (15 to 20 cm) wide and 1 to 2 in (2.5 to 5 cm) shorter than the finished width of the quilt at the top edge.
■ Hem the ends of the fabric strip, fold it in half lengthwise, wrong sides together, and sew the long, raw edges together with a ¼ in (6 mm) seam.
■ Fold the tube so that the seam is centered on one side and press the seam open.
■ Place the tube on the back of the quilt, just over the binding at the top, with the side with the seam against the quilt.

■ Hand sew the top edge of the sleeve to the quilt, taking care not to catch the front of the quilt as you stitch.
■ Push the front side of the tube up so that the top edge covers about half of the binding. This will provide a little 'give' so that when the quilt is hung the rod does not put strain on the quilt.
■ Sew the bottom edge of the sleeve in place.
■ Slide a curtain rod, a piece of wooden dowel or a lath through the sleeve. The seam on the back of the sleeve will keep the rod from coming in direct contact with the quilt.
■ To hang the quilt from a wall, suspend the rod on brackets, or attach screw eyes or drill holes at each end of the rod and slip the holes or eyes over small nails inserted in the wall.

Feathered Fancy

The quilt's central panel contains heart-shaped feather patterns. Cables are quilted around the outside edges.

This whitework 'fancy' quilt is named after its central quilting pattern, a heart-shaped feather. It is created from light, pre-washed cotton fabric and quilted by machine using free motion and walking foot techniques.

Finished size For a single bed (135 x 200 cm; 53 x 79 in)

Materials
◆ 7 yd (6.4 meters) pre-washed white cotton fabric (includes backing and binding)
◆ Batting to fit
◆ Monofilament thread
◆ White general purpose sewing thread
◆ Water-soluble blue ink marking pen
◆ Black permanent marking pen
◆ Sheet of white paper
◆ Unwaxed greaseproof paper
◆ Ruler
◆ Safety pins
◆ Sewing machine
◆ Darning foot or quilting foot
◆ Walking foot

CUTTING AND PREPARATION

1 From the length of pre-washed fabric, cut a 79 in (2 m) length for the top of the quilt and a 87 in (2.2 m) length for the backing. Cut a second 87 in (2.2 m) length of fabric and cut this length into strips parallel to the selvage referring to the Cutting the Fabric diagram below. Cut off all the selvage edges and join a 6½ in (165 mm) strip to each side of the quilt top and a 8½ in (216 mm) strip to each side of the quilt back. Press the seams open. Lay out the quilt top and, using a blue water-soluble pen, lightly mark a ¾ in (19 mm) line from each edge of the top. Mark another rectangle 12 in (305 mm) inside this line. These two marked rectangles will act as guides when transferring the cable patterns.

Four strips 2¼ in wide for quilt binding

8½ in	8½ in	6½ in	6½ in
Quilt back	Quilt back	Quilt top	Quilt top

2.2 m

Cut at 2 m mark

RIGHT The whitework quilt is useful as a throw rug or makes an impressive covering for the bed in a visitor's room.

2 Find the center of the quilt top, both vertically and horizontally, and mark these two lines within the inner rectangle. These lines will act as guides when transferring the feathered heart patterns.

3 Cut pieces of greaseproof paper long enough for each side of the quilt and two pieces for both the top and bottom of the quilt (see sheet A of the fold-out sheets in the back of this book). Trace the Cable Pattern onto this paper using a permanent marking pen. Each side outer cable has ten cable repeats and the top and bottom outer cables have six cable repeats. Also trace four corner cables, joining the paper together with sticky tape. Repeat the same process for the inner cable, noting that there are six cable repeats on the sides and two cable repeats on the top and bottom.

4 Lay the traced out Cable Pattern underneath the white quilt top and, using the blue water-soluble marking lines as guides for the outer edges of the cables, pin it carefully in place. Draw the cables onto the quilt top, using the blue water-soluble pen. For accurate placement, it is best to work from the center out to the corners. After marking the outer cable, repeat to mark the inner cable.

5 Trace the Heart Pattern onto a sheet of white paper using a black marking pen. Using the quilt photograph as a guide, pin the Heart Pattern paper underneath the quilt top and trace the patterns using a blue water-soluble pen. The center line that has been marked on the quilt top will help you position the four hearts. Trace the center hearts approximately 2½ in (63 mm) from the center of the quilt facing in opposite directions. Trace another heart in the same direction, approximately 1½ in (38 mm) from the lower edge of the center hearts. In each of the corners of the center panel, trace another heart using only the inner feathers and the top little heart shape. Along each side of the center panel edges, trace three small heart shapes.

6 Mark a 1¾ in (45 mm) diagonal grid between the two cables using a ruler and the blue water-soluble pen. Mark another ¼ in (6 mm) line on the right side of each line or, to save you a little time, sew the second line without marking by using the edge of the walking foot as a guide or by altering the position of the needle.

QUILTING

7 Layer the quilt backing, batting and top together and pin the three layers. The cables are worked first, using monofilament thread in the top of the machine and regular sewing thread in the bobbin. A walking foot can be used for the cables. If you are confident with free motion quilting you may wish to use a quilting or darning foot and the free motion method. To sew free motion, drop or cover the feed dogs on the machine and set the stitch length to 0. If the machine has a pressure dial, reduce the pressure. The tension may have to be reduced a little, to prevent the bobbin thread from showing on the top of the work. Use a quilting or darning foot. When free motion quilting, it is best to avoid stopping and starting. To start stitching, bring the lower thread to the top of the work, and holding both threads, stitch approximately ten tiny stitches very closely together. Then trim the tails of both threads. When you have finished stitching, stitch another lot of tiny stitches to lock off the work. Start with the feathered hearts at the center of the little top heart and stitch around it. Then sew the loop and the bottom and the inner feathers on the right side. When you reach the lowest right side feather, stitch back following the spine line and continue stitching the outer right side feathers. At this point, sew over previously sewn stitches, stitching the left side feathers in the same order. It is well worth the time to make a small quilt sandwich to practise free motion quilting before beginning on the quilt. Don't forget to reset the sewing machine for general sewing when you have finished. When both cables and feathers have been sewn, change to a walking foot and stitch the diagonal lines. Use a stitch length of approximately 2.5 to 3 to stitch these lines, again locking work off by starting and stopping with tiny stitches.

BINDING

8 Join the four 2¼ in (57 mm) wide strips with 45 degree angles to make one long strip and press the seams open. Press the length of binding in half, wrong sides together. Using a ¼ in (6 mm) seam, stitch the binding around the edge of the quilt, with all raw edges even and mitring at each corner. Trim the excess batting and backing fabric to approximately ¼ in (6 mm) beyond the edge of the quilt top. Roll the binding to the back of the quilt and hand stitch in place. Wash the quilt carefully to remove the blue lines. Add a label.

The pristine white cotton fabric is the perfect medium to show off the intricate feather and cable quilting patterns.

Dainty Pink Dresden Plate

The Dresden Plate block, also known as the Friendship Ring and the Aster block, combines patchwork and appliqué techniques. It is a good scrap bag pattern.

Pastel prints are used in this appealing variation of the Dresden Plate block. The prints are pretty and feminine, making the quilt perfect for a little girl's bedroom. The Dresden Plate block is easily pieced together and then appliquéd onto a background square.

Size For a single bed (140 x 229 cm; 55 x 90 in)

Materials*

◆ 19⅝ in (50 cm) of fabric with a white print background
◆ 39⅜ in (1 m) of fabric with a pink check background
◆ 29½ in (75 cm) of fabric with a light pink check for the sides
◆ 9⅞ in (25 cm) of two different white prints**
◆ 19⅝ in (50 cm) of two different light pink prints (A prints)**
◆ 9⅞ in (25 cm) of another two different light pink prints (B prints)**

LEFT The pretty scalloped edges, finished with pink binding fabric, are a feature of this quilt. They are designed to fall neatly over the sides of a bed, to rest just above the floor.

◆ 19⅝ in (50 cm) of fabric for the first border and the centers

◆ 2¾ yd (2.5 m) of fabric for the second border

◆ 3⅞ yd (3.5 m) of backing fabric

◆ 1¾ yd (1.6 m) of 3¼ yd (3 meter) wide continuous wadding or single (twin) size batting

◆ 10 yd (9 m) of binding

◆ 2¼ yd (2 m) of Vylene

◆ Cardboard or plastic for templates

* Laura Ashley prints were used for the quilt photographed. These fabrics are generally 54 in (140 cm) wide, but the calculations here are based on 42 in (112 cm) wide fabrics.

** If the prints are directional, use double the quantity given, to enable you to match up the pattern.

CUTTING THE FABRIC

Note: Cut all fabric selvage to selvage.

1 Starting with the white print background fabric, cut a piece 12½ in (318 mm) long. Crosscut into three 12½ in (318 mm) squares.

2 From the pink check background fabric, cut three 12½ in (318 mm) strips. Crosscut into eight 12½ in (318 mm) squares.

3 From the light pink check fabric cut a 18¼ in (464 mm) strip. Crosscut this into two 18¼ in (464 mm) squares. Cut each square twice diagonally from corner to corner to make eight quarter-square side triangles. Cut a 9⅜ in (238 mm) strip. Cut this into two 9⅜ in (238 mm) squares then cut each square once diagonally from corner to corner to make four half-square corner triangles.

4 Using the Plate Petal Template opposite, cut thirty-two petals from each of the white prints.

5 Using the Plate Petal Template, cut forty-four petals from each of the light pink A prints. Then use the template to cut twelve petals from each of the light pink B prints.

6 From the first border fabric, cut six 2½ in (63 mm) strips. Join two 2½ in (63 mm) strips together, using a diagonal seam, to make a continuous length. Repeat this procedure using another two 2½ (63 mm) strips. Using the Center Template opposite cut eleven centers.

7 From the second border fabric, cut four 10½ x 98 in (267 mm x 249 cm) lengths down the fabric (parallel to the selvage). Trim two of the 10½ x 98 in (267 mm x 249 cm) lengths back to 10½ x 65 in (267 mm x 165 cm).

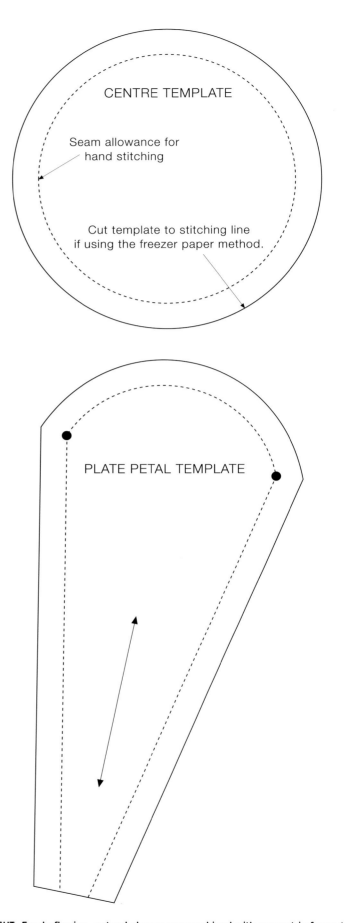

CENTRE TEMPLATE

Seam allowance for hand stitching

Cut template to stitching line if using the freezer paper method.

PLATE PETAL TEMPLATE

RIGHT Freely flowing, natural shapes are combined with geometric forms to create an appealing, varied design. Pink, green and white fabrics in florals and checks provide charming color contrasts.

8 From the backing fabric, cut a 96 in length (see the diagram below). Also cut two 20 in lengths. Join the 20 in lengths together end to end and then sew the joined lengths to one side of the 96 in length. Cut off the excess fabric and iron all the seams open.

JOINING THE BACKING FABRIC

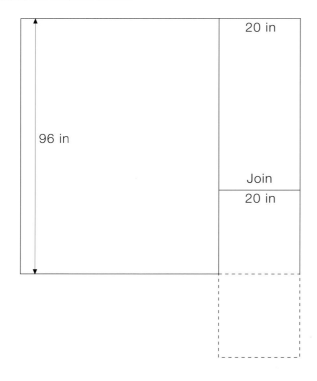

9 Cut the batting down to a 60 x 96 in rectangle or join pieces together to make it this size.

SEWING THE BINDING FABRIC

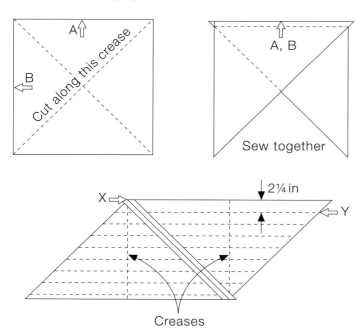

10 Working from the selvage edge on one side of the binding fabric, cut out a 35 in (89 cm) square (or use the length of the fabric to determine the same width). Fold the square in half diagonally in each direction and press a crease in each of the folds. Cut along one diagonal crease. Sew two halves together with a ¼ in (6 mm) seam. Press the seam open. With a ruler mark lines in 2¼ in (57 mm) widths across the binding strip. With right sides together and using a ¼ in (6 mm) seam, sew the binding strip to form a tube so that points X and Y on the diagram opposite match and the drawn lines are in alignment. Iron the seam open. Then cut along the drawn line, which will appear to be continuous. Iron the prepared length in half, wrong sides together, down the entire length of the bias strip. Prepare a label and a sleeve for hanging the quilt. Use the leftover piece of backing.

MAKING THE PLATES

11 Collect the thirty-two petals from both of the white prints and thirty-two of the petals from both of the light pink A prints, making sure that all the petals have the dots from the template marked on the wrong side of the petal. Split the petals into groups of four so that you have eight groups of four petals in each color group.

12 Take the groups of four petals in each of the four color groups and place them in alternating color order so that you have in the first pile the white print fabric, in the second pile the first light pink A print, in the third pile the second white print fabric and in the fourth pile the second light pink A print.

13 Take a petal from the first pile and a petal from the second pile and place right sides together (with the wrong side of the petal from the second pile to the top), matching the marked dots. Sew the petals together from the dot, reinforcing the stitch, down towards the center. Iron the seam open. Repeat with the other petals from the first and second piles until you have four pairs. (Starting at the scalloped edge, at the dot on the template, and sewing towards the center will result in neater plates and will make sewing easier.)

14 Repeat the process outlined in the step above with the petals from the third and fourth pile (with the wrong side of the petal to the top), until you have four pairs. Then join a pair of petals from the first and second piles to a pair from the third and fourth piles, with the wrong side of the petal pair from the third and fourth piles to the top. Again match the dots and sew from the dot to the center. Iron the seams open. Repeat until you have four sets.

15 Join two sets of petals made in the previous step to make a set of eight. Iron the seams open. Make two sets. Sew the two sets together to make a plate. Iron the seams open.

16 With Vylene to the right side of the Dresden Plate sections and using a ¼ in (6 mm) foot on the machine as a guide, stitch two sections together going around the scalloped edge from dot to dot. Trim the seam allowance to approximately ¹⁄₁₆ in (1.6 mm) wide and clip the curved edges where necessary.

17 Slash the Vylene in the center. Using this opening, turn the Dresden Plate to the right side. Iron flat. Iron the 12½ in pink check background square in half vertically, horizontally and diagonally. Use these creases to line up the plate on the background square and then appliqué the plate in place. Then appliqué the center circle over the open seams in the center.

DRESDEN PLATE

18 To make the three plates on the white background, gather the twelve petals in both the light pink B prints, and the remaining twelve petals in both the light pink A prints, making sure that all the petals have the dots from the template marked on the wrong side.

19 Split the petals into groups of four so that you have three groups of four petals in each color group. Take the groups of four petals in each of the four color groups and place in alternating color order so that you have in the first pile light pink B prints, in the second pile light pink A prints, in the third pile light pink B prints and in the fourth pile light pink A prints.

20 Following the procedure outlined in Steps 13 to 16, make the three plates. Sew them to the white background print squares following the procedure outlined in Step 17.

ASSEMBLING THE QUILT TOP

21 Sew a quarter-square light pink check triangle to both sides of a pink check background Dresden Plate block (see the diagram on page 92) as shown. Make two units. Sew a half-square light pink check triangle to the top of the unit. Make two of these units (unit 1). Sew a quarter-square light pink check triangle to a pink check background Dresden Plate block to a white background Dresden Plate block to a pink check background Dresden Plate block to a half-square light pink check triangle (unit 2). Make two units. Then sew unit 1 to unit 2. Make two of these (unit 3). Sew a quarter-square light pink check triangle to a pink check background Dresden Plate block, to a white background Dresden Plate block, to a pink check background Dresden Plate block, to a quarter-square light pink check triangle (unit 4). Sew one unit 3 to unit 4 to the second unit 3.

MAKING THE BORDERS

22 Mark the center of a 2½ in (63 mm) first border length and match it to the center of a 10½ x 65 in (267 mm x 165 cm) second border length (see the Stitching Borders diagram on page 93). Stitch together to form a top border length. Repeat the procedure to make a border for the bottom of the quilt top.

23 Match the center join of a joined 2½ in (63 mm) first border length with the center of a 10½ x 98 in (267 mm x 249 cm) border. Stitch together to make a side border length. Repeat to make a border for the other side of the quilt top. Sew the joined top border length to the top of the quilt top and the bottom border length to the bottom of the quilt top, making sure that you center the borders to the quilt top and that you sew the border onto the quilt top starting and finishing (with a reinforcing stitch) ¼ in (6 mm) in from the edge of the quilt top (see the Attaching Borders to Quilt Top diagram below). Sew the border lengths to the sides of the quilt top following the same procedure. Mitre the four corners of the borders.

ASSEMBLING THE QUILT

24 Test the marking pen or pencil on a scrap of the background fabric before marking the quilt top. Using a quilting pattern of your choice, mark all the side and

SEWING TRIANGLES TO PLATE BLOCK

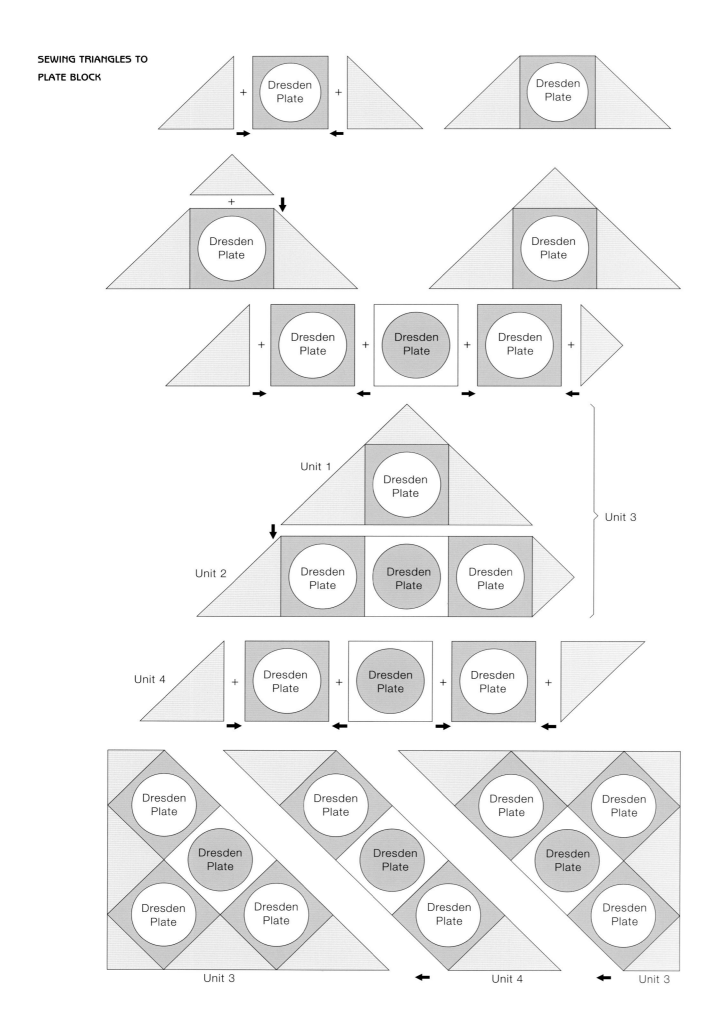

corner triangles in the center of the quilt top. Using the diagonal seam lines of the blocks in the main part of the quilt top, draw diagonal lines radiating out from the center of the quilt in 2 in (50 mm) intervals. Using the Curved Edge Template on sheet A of the fold-out sheets in the center of this book, draw in the rounded edge on the quilt top but do not cut it out at this stage.

QUILTING

25 Layer the quilt backing, batting and top. Quilt in the ditch around all the blocks and borders. Then quilt the drawn diagonal lines in the border. Finally, quilt in the ditch around each plate and each petal in the plate. Quilt around the centers of all the plates. Quilt each pattern in the side and the corner triangles in the center of the quilt top.

BINDING

26 After the quilt top has been quilted, go over the drawn scalloped edge with the pattern and reshape it where necessary. The quilting may have distorted the edge of the quilt and it is better to reshape now. When the edge has been reshaped, stitch a running stitch ⅛ in (3 mm) in from the drawn line and then cut on the drawn line. With the raw edges of the binding matching the raw edge of the quilt, sew the 2¼ in (57 mm) continuous bias length that has been ironed in half, wrong sides together down the entire length, to the quilt. Hand or machine stitch in place. Stitch the label and the sleeve for hanging the quilt.

STITCHING BORDERS

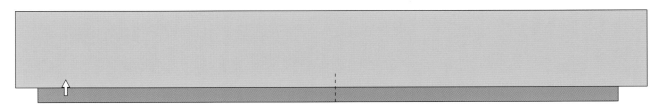

ATTACHING BORDERS TO QUILT TOP

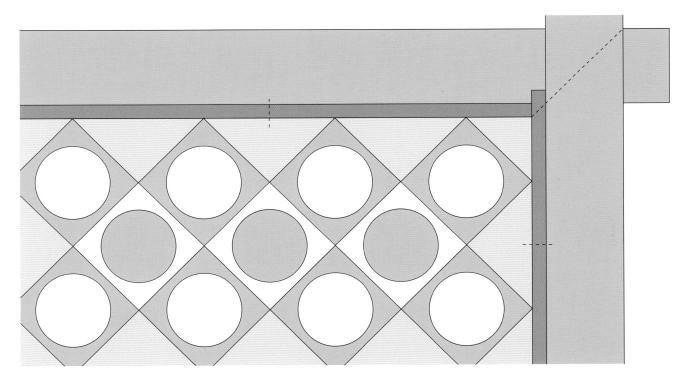

Index

Thunder Bay Press
An imprint of the Advantage Publishers Group
THUNDER BAY 5880 Oberlin Drive, San Diego, CA 92121-4794
P · R · E · S · S www.thunderbaybooks.com

ISBN-13: 978-1-59223-575-9
ISBN-10: 1-59223-575-1

Printed by Sing Cheong Printing Co., Ltd.
Printed in CHINA
1 2 3 4 5 10 09 08 07 06
Printed 2006